1990

University of St. Francis

S0-BNH-560

3 0301 00079639 7

Starting Out WELL

A PARENTS' APPROACH TO PHYSICAL ACTIVITY & NUTRITION

Helen T. Fish, MEd
Enota School, Gainesville, Georgia

Ronald B. Fish, BS
Northeast Georgia Medical Center

Lawrence A. Golding, PhD
University of Nevada, Las Vegas

LIBRARY
College of St. Francis
JOLIET, ILLINOIS

Leisure Press
Champaign, Illinois

This is dedicated to the ones we love.
All our love to Eric, Angie, Christie,
   and all the growing children of the world;
Brandon, Lisa, Scott, Neal, Kirk,
   and all the grown-up children;
Our mentors, Diane, Jim, Lu, Bob, Ellen, and Fran,
   who parented along with us; and
Our beautiful parents and siblings, who started it all.

Library of Congress Cataloging-in-Publication Data

Fish, Helen T., 1944-
   Starting out well : a parents' approach to physical activity and
   nutrition / Helen T. Fish, Ronald B. Fish, Lawrence A. Golding.
      p.   cm.
   Bibliography: p.
   Includes index.
   ISBN: 0-88011-346-4
   1. Children--Nutrition.   2. Exercise for children.   I. Fish,
Ronald B., 1942-   . II. Golding, Lawrence Arthur, 1926-
III. Title.
RJ206.F49   1989   88-26805
649'.3--dc19   CIP

ISBN: 0-88011-346-4

Copyright © 1989 by Helen Fish, Ron Fish, Lawrence A. Golding

All rights reserved. Except for use in a review, the reproduction or utilization
of this work in any form or by any electronic, mechanical, or other means,
now known or hereafter invented, including xerography, photocopying and
recording, and in any information retrieval system, is forbidden without the
written permission of the publisher.

Cover photo and inside photos by Travis Massey, Master of Photography,
Gainesville, GA. Photo of Lawrence A. Golding courtesy of Cheri Lynn
Studios, Las Vegas, NV. "Sugar Yukkies" logo on page 110 created by
Barbara Cook.

Developmental Editor: Lisa Busjahn
Managing Editor: Holly Gilly
Copyeditor: Peter Nelson
Proofreader: Phaedra Hise
Production Director: Ernie Noa
Typesetter: Brad Colson
Text Design: Keith Blomberg
Text Layout: Denise Mueller
Cover Design: Jack Davis
Illustrations By: Mary Yemma Long
Printed By: Versa Press

Printed in the United States of America

10 9 8 7 6 5 4 3 2 1

Leisure Press
A Division of Human Kinetics Publishers, Inc.
Box 5076, Champaign, IL 61825
1-800-342-5457
1-800-334-3665 (in Illinois)

649.3
F532

Contents

136,182

Preface

Current research on the impact of unhealthy lifestyles suggests the need for a revised look at the chubby baby image largely accepted as healthy. We need to include our children in activity and nutrition programs similar to those we so avidly seek for ourselves. Guided movement exploration and nutrition beginning in infancy will lead to a greater number of healthy and able adults. The family culture plays an important role in who and what people become—physically, mentally, and emotionally.

Having each worked in health, wellness, preschool, and early childhood fields for over 20 years, we have witnessed the detrimental effects of poor early lifestyles on later quality of life and health. We have noted that while many adults have developed a growing concern for their own wellness, many parents are unconsciously neglecting their children's healthful development in a phase of life when many health habits begin—from birth through kindergarten. If you think this is not true, just ask yourself how many times you have seen parents substituting a fat-laden french fry for the teething biscuit of days gone by.

Starting Out Well is designed to give parents and educators concrete ways to enhance lifestyles for today's infants, toddlers, and preschoolers—the healthy adults of the 21st century. Today's kindergartners will graduate in that enlightened century.

Throughout the book, we delineate age groups according to the National Research Council's Food and Nutritional Guidelines:

- Infants: Birth to 1 year of age
- Toddlers: 1 to 3 years of age
- Preschoolers: 3 years of age through kindergarten

Parents and educators should realize that these are only guides, not rigid classifications.

This book draws on child-rearing knowledge and practices from the past, discards what is harmful and unnecessary, then adds what we have learned about wellness through space-age technology.

Part I of this book, "Setting the Stage for an Active Life," will help you develop active ways to spend quality time with your child. This section includes specific, proper—yet fun—physical activities for each phase of early development—infant, toddler, and preschooler. The philosophy and exercises found in these four chapters were developed by Dr. Larry Golding, director of the Exercise Physiology Laboratory of the University of Nevada; Helen Fish, early childhood and pre-reading consultant for the Research and Development Center of the University of Wisconsin; and Ron Fish, director of wellness for the Northeast Georgia Medical Center and director of the Y's Ways to Physical Fitness Workshops, which have trained thousands of fitness specialists.

In Part II, "Making Good Nutrition a Lifelong Habit," you will learn specific ways to provide nutritional choices for your child. The recipes come from the booklet *From Our Hearts, For Your Heart* compiled by Helen Fish, who gathered healthful recipes from hundreds of mothers every February, Heart Health Month, for 15 years. These recipes were then edited by Dale Wilson, a registered dietician, and analyzed for such nutritional content as calories, protein, carbohydrates, fat, sodium, and cholesterol. Thus, the recipes are "mother approved" for appeal and "nutritionally approved" by a dietician specializing in children's wellness.

Parents and all others involved in early childhood education play a significant part in the phases of children's growth and development. What we do with our children in the physical realm affects their intellectual, social, and emotional development. There is not one right way to nurture. Instead, we grow as the child grows. Rather than feeling guilt for what we do that isn't perfect, we can experience the joy in mutual learning. We try again, and our children learn the value of persistence. At times we feel inadequate for a task or frustrated by our lack of patience. Yet we need to continue to value our own growth as we find more ways of allowing our growing children their own uniqueness. We should continually nurture and value the love that exists between us and our children. If we do this, we will have helped our children grow as whole children, not merely as a sum of all their parts.

The solution to physical inactivity and obesity lies with the development of healthy lifestyles beginning in infancy. *Starting Out Well* presents a philosophy of child-rearing that fosters physical fitness and normal body weight through interesting, challenging physical activities and a sensible, sound diet. A child is naturally active, and this activity should be guided and directed, not stifled. Sitting still feels unnatural. Physically active children are also hungry children, and this eager appetite should be led down the path of exciting, good nutrition.

Acknowledgments

To the many professionals who supported us in this creation. We especially acknowledge: William T. Langston, MD, pediatrician and wellness consultant, who reviewed the entire text for medical accuracy; Dale M. Wilson, RD, who reviewed hundreds of recipes to find the best, and then analyzed them for nutritional content; John H. Berg, MD, who has watched over our family's wellness through the years; William D. Saul, MD, Obstetrics and Gynecology at Goddard Hospital and Tufts University; John A. Ferguson, John K. Pharr, and Greg N. Robinson, the administrative staff at Northeast Georgia Medical Center, who support the ideals and concrete applications of wellness; Shirley W. Whitaker, Principal of Enota School in Gainesville, Georgia; William B. Ware, PhD, Dean of the College of Education at Brenau College in Gainesville, Georgia; and Sue Wilmoth, PhD and William Zuti, PhD.

PART I

Setting the Stage for an Active Life

The time is right for parents to replace the verbal command "Sit still" with "Let's all get up and move." Scientific and popular literature both support the benefits of enhanced physical fitness. As a parent you have a choice: to spend time and energy finding ways to help your child explore her environment or to let her adopt a sedentary lifestyle.

As a parent you need to realize your influence and impact in helping your child establish an active lifestyle. In addition, you need to become more aware of and involved with others who conduct programs in which your child takes part.

Examining the benefits of adopting a "moving" lifestyle is what Part I is all about. In chapter 1 we take a look at children's natural inclination to move and explore the environment. How physical activity is linked to intellectual and emotional growth is also addressed. Chapter 2 looks at social factors, such as TV and modern transportation, that discourage physical activity and make it easy for parents and children to adopt sedentary lifestyles. You need alternatives to having your child sit still; several suggestions are given in chapters 3 and 4. You'll find these exercises easy to do as well as beneficial. Enjoy "moving" with your child.

Chapter 1

A Child's Natural Inclination to Move

"Sit still!!" How many times have you heard this phrase? Was it directed at you in school, in the car, at the table, at all adult gatherings? How many times have you used this phrase with your own child? How many times was it justified?

This phrase has merit in its rightful place. However, the frequency of its use is questionable. When should it be used? What goes before and after its use?

To grow and develop to their fullest capacity, children should be allowed to move and explore. If you help your child exercise and you make the experience a pleasurable activity that will last a lifetime, your child's development patterns can be maximized. You should allow her to move whenever the opportunity arises, rather than repress the innate need to move. Indeed, movement is one of the first signals that there is "new life" when the child is developing in the uterus. This inherent, basic need should be encouraged throughout life rather than repressed.

The terms *infant, toddler*, and *preschooler* are used throughout this book as we name, define, and explore activities for each of the broad developmental stages from birth to grade-school age. Each stage is unique and different, and each phase builds upon the preceding stages.

Let us refer to the following definitions as we study the early stages of child development:

1. Infancy stage: from birth to 1 year of age.
2. Toddler stage: from 1 to 3 years of age.
3. Preschool stage: from 3 years through kindergarten.

Note: This final stage generally is completed at 6 years of age, but it is recognized that there is much variety of ages as to when children complete kindergarten and commence grade school. The following principles and practices are appropriate through the kindergarten year and have even been used successfully with primary grade children.

Growth and Development

Consider the tremendous learning and growth that occur between birth and 5 years of age. Begin to consider the phenomenal changes in physical development by reviewing a facet of development with which everyone is familiar—language acquisition. Comparably marvelous development will then be found in the children's physical prowess.

Language Development

Before your child's first birthday, her language develops from a stage of random babbling to back-and-forth babbling with adults. She then progresses toward the remarkable activity of recognizing words for familiar parts of the environment, such as *mama, daddy,* and her own simple words for familiar objects. At approximately 1 year of age, your infant can follow simple requests and begins to develop a speaking vocabulary. Normally, by the age of 2, your toddler's speaking vocabulary has expanded to 15 to 30 words; amazingly, by 5, it has *exploded* to over 2,000 words. This tremendous growth in vocabulary comes naturally and easily under the tutelage of your child's first and potentially best teacher—you, her parent.

Physical Development

This growth in language is paralleled by equally amazing changes in physical development during this same time period. Consider your newborn infant who emerges from the womb virtually helpless.

Cephalocaudal Trend

Early in development, your infant is able to turn her head from side to side. She begins to reach out and grasp for objects as improved muscle coordination progresses from her head down the central nervous system (development is *cephalocaudal*: from head to tail). Thus, head control is first, followed by arm control, and, lastly, muscular control in the legs.

The cephalocaudal trend encourages a parent aware of child development to first elicit the baby's head-turning with a strategically placed mirror or toy, followed by promoting eye-hand activities with numerous rattles, and so on. Your 20-week-old infant's eyes are alert, yet her trunk is still so flaccid that she must be propped up to maintain a sitting position; Unassisted sitting, standing, and walking will build on this earlier stage.

Proximodistal Development

Your infant's control also expands from her central core to her outer extremities. This type of development is referred to as *proximodistal*: from near to far. Wide-range use of her arms comes before fingertip control. And so your child in her natural state kicks for the pure pleasure of movement. She begins to sit with support at about 6 months of age. As her back strengthens, she learns to balance, first with awkward, random jerks, later with a smoothness that makes it hard to detect that an act of balancing once had to be worked on with difficulty.

Development of Walking Skills

As strength and coordination of limbs develop, your infant learns to roll from back to front and from abdomen to back. Hand coordination increases as she learns to shake rattles and even to move objects from one hand to another. More remarkable physical developments continue, as she is gradually able to support her own weight when held in a standing position.

Meanwhile, your baby has learned to rise up on all fours and, when enticed by a desirable object placed in front of her, begins to scoot forward. Scooting is gradually replaced by a definite alternating-leg approach to crawling, until finally she has mastered the fine art of crawling with lightning speed. In fact, some children become so delighted with the speed at which they can get around that they are satisfied with crawling—for the time being, that is. Soon, or concurrently, your infant is mastering pulling herself up on low, sturdy objects to a full standing position. She is growing in independence as well as physical coordination. Thus, her cephalocaudal and proximodistal trends continue to develop as she approaches the rather distinctly human skill of walking in an upright position.

Your child again begins with a supporting friend, usually a parent, as she tries inching along furniture. Then she continues to try it out on her own until she begins to test her newfound coordination, which extends all the way down to her toes. This balance even includes the arms and fingertips, as she masters that first independent step. The walking act becomes more complex and refined. She gradually learns to move with quickness and ease, until she is finally able to run.

Continued Development of Complex Skills

Other remarkable physical skills continue to evolve. By 5 years of age, your child has developed the ability to bounce and throw a ball, to jump over a rope, to carry a heavy object, to use a sled, to ride a two-wheeled bike with training wheels, to roll down a hill, and to do a somersault. In addition, hand-eye coordination, fine muscle coordination, social skills, and self-care have also developed.

The Important Habit of Physical Activity

These early years are the time to establish habits that will last a lifetime. The importance of children's building habits of physical activity for health problem prevention is well known. The literature is replete with the proven benefits of movement-oriented, physical interaction with the environment. Articles extolling these benefits not only repeatedly appear in newspapers and magazines but also in professional journals. The *Morbidity and Mortality Weekly Report* (Center for Disease Control, 1987) systematically reviews the medical literature. This review revealed that 43 English-language studies indicated that physical activity helps prevent coronary heart disease (CHD). Furthermore, the authors found that poor assessment methods used in previous studies had led to erroneous inferences of "no causal association" between activity and CHD prevention.

Besides protecting against coronary heart disease, increased levels of physical activity also protect against other chronic diseases (Siscovick, LaPorte, & Newman, 1985; Taylor, Sallis, & Needle, 1985). The Public Health Service's 1990 "Health Objectives for the Nation" include 11 objectives that relate to physical fitness and exercise (Public Health Service, 1980). Although these objectives call for regular, vigorous physical movement, less intensive (yet regular) physical activity is also beneficial (Sallis, Haskell, Fortmann, Wood, & Vranizan, 1985). There are so many physically inactive Americans that additional steps should be taken to promote a lifestyle that includes regularly scheduled physical activity (Iverson, Fielding, Crow, & Christenson, 1985). We believe this should start in infancy and become a lifelong habit.

The Role of Environment

In what kind of environment do the remarkable changes of early childhood take place? They take place on warm, sunny days and on cool, snug ones, on family room floors and in baby's crib. The environment for the greatest learning growth is flexible and changing. It has firm limits, but a wide variety of experiences within these limits. At times, the environment is confined, but mostly it is free flowing. And in what kind of atmosphere does all this flourish? In a loving but firm one—an atmosphere that is often noisy yet values time for quiet activities as well, one that encourages yet challenges the child. This includes an environment that encourages active playing, cuddling, and one-to-one contact.

The Enriched Environment

Your child's natural inclination in such an atmosphere is one of continual seeking and continuous growth. By allowing explorations that include movement, you can allow your child's intelligence quotient to rise by as much as 10 to 15 points (Moss & Kagan, 1958). Barbara Clark is a noted author on gifted children. Having reviewed the newer fields of psychobiology and brain-mind research, she provides insight on how to provide a more effective educational experience for children. She states, "The growth of intelligence depends on the interaction between our biological inheritance and our environmental opportunities to use that inheritance" (Clark, 1983, p. 6). Clark further relates that two children with the same approximate genetic program could turn out to be regarded either as high achieving and potentially gifted or as educably retarded, depending on the richness of the environment that each interacted with during the earliest years. Environmental interactions occur whether they are planned or unplanned. This interaction can result in a 20- to 40-point difference in measured intelligence (Bloom, 1964; Skeels & Dye, 1959; Hunt & Kirk, 1971).

Interactions in an enriched environment even change the chemical structure of the neural cell and allow information to be processed more quickly (Rosensweig, 1966; Brierly, 1976; Teyler, 1977; Clark, 1983). Thus, we change children at the raw cellular level, not just in the behavior outwardly exhibited. Clark (1983) summarizes children's potential for early intellectual growth like this:

> In this way gifted children become biologically different from average learners, not at birth, but as a result of using and developing the wondrous, complex structure with which they were born. At birth, nearly everyone is programmed to be phenomenal. (p. 21)

The preschool population is changing. The Stanford-Binet Intelligence Test had to be renormed upward to reflect a dramatic rise in IQ levels, especially among preschoolers. It might be assumed that both the higher education levels of parents and richer environments have helped foster this change. Clark (1983) states that this enriched environment includes such factors as higher mobility as well as wider use of educational toys and books, television, and better nutrition.

The Deprived Environment

Let us now view a real-life example of what can happen when the child is *not* allowed to move, explore, and expand his environment. Danny is a 4-year-old boy, barely verbal and not quite toilet trained. He literally clings to any person who comes into his environment.

Danny's mother had already raised a family. She married a second time and had Danny later in life. Partly so that Danny would be safe from all her pins and needles (she worked at home as a seamstress) and partly because he distracted her from the work she wanted to accomplish, the mother would place him in his playpen for several hours at a time. She put a large, heavy door across the top of it so that he would stop trying to get out. Other times, he was locked in his room, where, although he did have a number of pretty toys, he had no human companionship.

Can it be any wonder that when any stranger visited Danny's home, Danny would literally hang on to this person? Subsequent years in school reflected his early childhood deprivation: Danny had learning problems and an inability to relate to peers. He hadn't been allowed to expand and explore either his environment or human relationships.

A final affirmation of an interactive approach to intelligence is reflected in the words of neurobiologist T. Teyler (1977):

> The fabric of the brain is set down as a result of the interaction of genetic blueprints and environmental influences. While the basic features of brain organization are present at birth (cell division is essentially complete), the brain experiences tremendous growth in neural processes, synapse formation and myelin sheath formation, declining about puberty. These processes can be profoundly altered by the organism's environment. Furthermore, it has been shown that brain processes present at birth will degenerate if the environmental stimulation necessary to activate them is withheld. It appears that the genetic contribution provides a framework which, if *not* used, will disappear, but which is capable of further development given the optimal environmental stimulation. (pp. 31-32)

Consider another real-life example to illustrate these ideas: Tim, age 5, came to kindergarten appearing uncared for. His clothes were dirty and smelled of urine. He exhibited unusual behavior: He continually wanted to touch, smell, bite, and eat everything in the classroom that he could get his hands on.

A home visit helped clarify his behavior and learning problems. Tim had been active as an infant and toddler. His mother, with a 6th-grade education and few parenting skills, became so frustrated by his hyperactivity that she would not allow him to play outdoors. This only made his need to move worse. She then began locking him in his room. When this frustrated him, he threw things, so she removed everything but his mattress. Thus, he had a constant need to explore when he came to school.

In contrast, words seem inadequate to express the joy on the faces of infants, toddlers, and preschoolers as they explore their world in active ways. Their eyes light up as they chase a feather or clamber through a tire obstacle course. The delight on their faces is reflected in the proud and happy feelings seen on the mothers' and fathers' faces. The day is passing when mothers do the majority of the child-rearing; with so many working moms today, certain joyous moments of raising children are shared more equally between fathers and mothers. A special bonding continues to grow as Johnny tests his skills in precariously climbing up a slightly inclined ladder while Dad keeps a strong hand ready in case Johnny should slip. Mom also senses the trusting relationship as she extends just one finger for support while Jessica crosses the balance beam that is a few inches off the floor.

If only all parents could realize how important and vital they are to their children's development. For it is not only what they do to and with their children but also the manner in which it is done. Parents must not become overburdened when reflecting upon their awesome responsibility (or opportunity) in creating such expanding environments and their effects on their children's development. They should instead delight in every small act (playing peekaboo and so on) and be cognizant of how they really help their children learn. Parents can help children become "more" than what they were at birth, not more able to go beyond the limitations of their physical structures or inborn characteristics, but in their ability to use those characteristics and structures.

Parents and all early childhood educators need to instill in their children a lifestyle that includes regularly scheduled physical activity. By adding verbal interactions to the physical activity, parents help the children develop in more than one way. The environment influences the *total* child's growth. What is done and how it is done affects children

- physically, with more optimal and preventive health;
- mentally, with maximum intellectual growth due to positive interactions with the environment;
- emotionally, while parents and children interface, spending time, energy, talents, and involvement in interacting (as in the following chapters' activities), the children realize how much parents care, gaining deeper understanding of love.

Parents and educators need to be highly sensitive to the needs that children express as well as to their developmental levels. Parents will then be able to challenge and support this developing person. Without such efforts, intellectual, emotional, and physical abilities will be wasted, and untold potential will not come to full realization. The following chapters will include a variety of ideas to help you as you stimulate your child's *total* growth and development.

How Significant Others Influence Your Child

In today's world it is not only parents who play an important role in children's early development. There are many others who are likely to be working with children—grandparents, babysitters, volunteers and teachers at day-care centers or preschools, staff at recreation or Y programs, and Sunday school teachers. When you select an outside-the-home activity for your child, try to choose an environment that allows her to explore life mentally, spiritually, and physically.

Pleasurable, developmentally powerful physical activities should be enjoyed as a part of the child-parent partnership in all the early stages of child development. Whether you encourage head movement in the early cephalocaudal stage or, in later stages, encourage your child to sit or balance or, finally, to stand and walk, each encouraging "partner activity" helps your child develop to her fullest potential. Each partner is important in affecting your child's growth, whether it be a parent, a teacher, a grandparent, a relative, a neighbor, or a sibling.

You may be asking yourself how we authors raised our children. For example, did we use a playpen in raising our preschoolers? Well, the answer is "yes, occasionally." When your child is crawling, and a safe place is needed for a short period of time, the playpen is great. It enables you to go to another floor and quickly throw in a load of laundry. Sometimes, though, just take your child with you, whether in a backpack or in your arms. Don't leave your child in a playpen for an extended period of time just to get things done. There is a time for such mobility restriction (for safety or social reasons), but in your everyday life, you should think of your child's natural inclinations to explore, grow, and move, as she learns by these explorations and movements.

Chapter 2

Influences Inhibiting
a Child's Natural
Inclination to Move

In parents' desire to teach their children to be good, they risk inhibiting their physical exploration of the world. As you observe the endless activities and movements of your preschooler, you should be aware of the influences that may inhibit this natural curiosity. Some of these influences include social regulations, television, modern transportation, and the schools.

Social Regulations

"Johnny, be good!" This phrase is used so frequently that several years ago it even became the title of a popular song. Parents admonish children to be good. Being good usually means sitting still and keeping quiet. Parents reward children when they conform, and punish them when they do not. Certain behaviors are not only desirable but necessary, for without them civilized society could not exist.

People can, however, reexamine expectations of these behaviors according to children's stages of development. For example, parents can teach children to be quiet and still for a short period of time in a place of worship. However, parents can also consider the need for activity by doing such simple things as making sure their children have a few minutes of exercise both before and after the church service. In other words, if you take an 18-month-old from the high chair where he has been sitting during breakfast, cajole him to lie still while you dress him, carry him to the car, restrain him in his car seat, and transport him into church, can you possibly expect him to sit still in that pew for an hour? How simple it would be to allow enough extra time to give him a few minutes to roam about your house after you have dressed him, then let him walk to the car and into the church. Even if it does take just a little more time, adjusting your schedule to your child's stage of development can make it easier for the whole family, and certainly happier for the child.

The same principle can apply to other social functions where children's mobility must be limited, such as family dinners, eating in a restaurant, or going shopping. The grocery store or supermarket is a wondrous adventure for children, yet parents expect children to sit still in the shopping carts and behave like adults. In fact, watch parents discipline children in supermarkets: They expect these bundles of natural activity and curiosity to act adult and mature. What a waste of a fun time and a potential learning adventure.

A rule of thumb to remember is to try to provide a period of movement before and after a period in which you expect Johnny or Julie to be "good" or sit still.

Television and Young Children

Marie Winn's book The Plug-In Drug (1985) addresses the effects of television on children. Other authors have studied the effect of television on lowered national high school standardized test results. Television habits start with the young child. Television induces zombielike behavior in a majority of the preschoolers studied.

Most mothers recognize the babysitting capabilities of the television set. Just the flick of a switch will transform active and noisy children into tranquil and docile zombies. Parents call their names but they won't hear. They have tuned the parents out. They are being "good!" Parents then don't need to "interrupt" their activities to interact with their children, for they are intensely involved with something else. Parents can get tasks done—the kids are quiet, stationary, and engrossed.

Thus absorbed, children are "good," but is this good for them? Too much television can be harmful! You wouldn't let your children become addicted to any other bad habit, so be aware of the quantity and the quality of what they watch. We are not suggesting that there be no television, but rather that you be aware of its possible dangers and limit viewing time. Another suggestion is to watch the program *with* your child; then he interacts with another human's responses rather than just reacts to what he sees on the screen.

Family Lifestyle

The use of cars, buses, and other forms of transportation has greatly decreased the amount that people walk. People generally exert as little effort as possible to get from one place to another. How many times have you driven around and around a parking lot searching for the shortest distance from car to store? People seem to pointedly avoid the first form of transportation known to humans—walking.

Adults are becoming increasingly aware of the beneficial effects of exercise, and it is common to see them jogging, walking, or cycling. This need for exercise doesn't often seem to translate to the children of the family, though. Most often children are bused to and from school and are driven to almost every function that they attend.

Because children are not independent and must accompany adults, they are forced into mechanized transportation. What better activity could adults share with their children than including them in their exercise periods?

The Role of Schools

When children enter school, they are allowed some exploration and movement, especially in preschools, nursery schools, daycare centers, and even kindergartens. However, as children move up the academic ladder, this type of mobility and exploration is generally frowned upon and controlled. Children usually learn more skills before they enter school than at any other time in their lives, yet that natural quest for learning is too often squelched. Kindergartners generally love school, but do they sustain this love as they advance through the grades?

Many classrooms are arranged with desks in perfect rows, which fosters little interaction between children. In many classrooms the teacher talks 80 percent of the time, while the children are compelled to sit still.

It is known, however, that communication is accomplished through an active involvement with the environment. What an amazing accomplishment talking is! It allows people to communicate thoughts and feelings to others.

Your Child's Classroom

What kind of an educational atmosphere prevails in your child's classroom? Is there some freedom of movement and communication? It is much easier for the teacher to lecture "university style" than to use the ingenuity and creativity necessary in an "open" classroom. Become involved in your child's school and help promote freedom of movement and communication interspersed between periods of quiet. One of the bitter lessons a teacher learns while taking a college course is how hard it is to sit while the instructor lectures; you yourself might recall how hard it is to sit during a lengthy speech or meeting. Does your child's teacher remember how hard it is to sit still? Does the teacher then allow the children some freedom of movement?

Your Child's Physical Education Program

What type of physical education is offered, if any? The best way to find out is to visit the school. Do physical education classes really involve the children in active, aerobic workouts or is a great deal of the children's time spent answering roll call, waiting in line, or standing at the sidelines watching a few others move?

If your child's school PE program is like the one just described, become involved in your school to influence needed changes. All the children (and the teacher) should be actively moving.

Community Resources

Look for a variety of quality programs within the community. For example, many park and recreation departments and church groups offer a wide range of physical activities that would encourage your child to move. "Feelin' Good" is a YMCA program that "combines classroom instruction with aerobic workouts to put kids on the road to a lifetime of heart health." The benefits of this program are supported by a Jackson County, Michigan, study involving 24,000 children and funded by the W.K. Kellogg Foundation. The results showed that the children in the "Feelin' Good" program improved their aerobic fitness, lowered their blood pressure and cholesterol levels, and reduced their body fat (Boyer, 1984).

All of these changes are involved in the prevention of heart disease, and it is well documented that heart disease has its foundations in youth. Most authorities believe that good patterns of physical activity, eating, and other basic health concepts must be established early in life. The basic concepts of good health may be summarized as follows:

1. Be physically active.
2. Eat a prudent diet, including three balanced meals per day.
3. Maintain normal weight.
4. Avoid unhealthy habits, particularly smoking.
5. Get adequate sleep.
6. Be happy.

As a parent, you should be concerned with the kind of exercise your child is receiving and the type of health information he is learning.

Be an Involved Parent!

The school—and in particular, your child's teachers—is part of your child's life a great portion of his waking days. Become actively involved in situations that influence your child. Become involved with the school's PTA. Most teachers welcome the chance to work with parents. However, remember that *you* are your child's first and most influential teacher and that what you create and inspire *before* he enters school can and will last a lifetime!

Other factors inhibit children's natural inclination to move, explore, and learn, but the ones discussed—certain social behaviors, television, transportation, and school—are among the most important. We are not saying that these influences should be abolished or even that they are necessarily bad. Rather, we urge that a wise, tempered use of them be maintained. The school falls into a unique classification of being potentially one of the most important influences on the child, and it is therefore imperative that you as a parent know what is being taught within your schools.

Chapter 3

How to Encourage and Sustain a Love of Activity

To overcome the numerous factors limiting children's level of activity, adults need to devise alternate activities. For instance, you could encourage your child's mobility around the house, develop fun exercises for you and her to do together, and get involved in school, YMCA, or parks and recreation department programs.

Developing Your Infant's Mobility

You can encourage mobility and inquisitiveness in your child from early infancy. Remember that development starts with the head and continues downward and outward throughout the body until strength and coordination of the fingers and toes develop.

Encourage Eye and Head Movement

Encourage development of your infant's head and eyes by hanging a mobile above her head. You can easily make a mobile with a clothes hanger, brightly colored yarn, and cutout pictures. However, remember that the mobile can get boring after a while; vary the colors and the objects. When your infant eventually reaches up and pulls the mobile down, suspend it out of her reach, but close enough so she can respond to the colors and the objects and observe the changes brought about by movements of the air.

Enable Grasping

As your infant's development progresses and she becomes able to grasp objects, place a rattle in her hand. As her development continues, occasionally place the rattle just out of reach; the purpose is not to frustrate her, but to let her learn that by moving and reaching, she can grasp it. Once she grasps the rattle and moves her hand, a noise occurs, and she develops the concept of cause and effect. Offer her a variety of objects. She will notice that a paper bag makes a certain kind of noise, that a fuzzy animal feels soft, and a small block feels hard. Bring new and exciting objects into her environment daily. Remember, it may be just a wooden spoon to you, but to her, seeing it, feeling it, tasting it, and listening to the noise it makes when banged against different objects are brand new experiences. All her senses are awakening. Appeal to them all.

Spark Intellectual Development and Speech

While extending your infant's sensory and physical horizons, broaden her intellectual capabilities by doing something as simple as talking to her. As you hand her the wooden spoon, tell her about it, how it feels, and what she can do with it. Introduce new objects to her as frequently as possible. Don't talk to her in baby talk. Instead, speak correctly, in complete sentences, and face-to-face. She will understand much of what you say to her long before she can verbally communicate back to you.

By using proper English, you can prevent some undesirable speech patterns. Take Jim, for example. By the time he was 4, he had acquired an extensive vocabulary, which included comprehensive use of compound sentences, accurate use of descriptive adjectives such as *remarkable* and *microscopic*, and the use of similes and metaphors such as "high as the mountains." Jim was also able to read and spell several words. Yet he retained a few undesirable language habits from his early language development. He would, for example, pronounce Vs as Bs, saying "berry well" instead of "very well." Jim's mother, recalling his early language development, realized she had unconsciously reinforced such immature patterns by being amused by them rather than trying to correct them. Jim eventually corrected his bad habits, but only with considerable effort.

Because children learn to speak by imitation, speak to your child in complete sentences from early infancy on. If your child uses an incorrect sound or word form, simply repeat the sentence using the correct form instead of making an issue out of it. For example, your child may say, "I doed it. I got the wagon in the garage." Simply say, "You did it! You got the wagon in the garage. I did see you." If you correct her in this manner, she won't feel condemned for her mistake. Instead, you used a grammatically correct reiteration of her statement. Notice that *doed* is a rather logical past-tense form of "do"—your child was applying a general past-tense formulation quite correctly. At this point in her speech development, she can't be expected to know all the irregularities of our language.

You expand your child's tactile and physical environment with care and imagination. Remember to talk to her frequently, and you will also expand her auditory, oral, and intellectual skills.

Create Awareness in Various Surroundings

Until your child is able to sit by herself and move around independently, change her location and position frequently. This repositioning expands her horizons. Rather than leave her in her crib all day, place her in an infant seat, swing, or port-a-crib during some of her waking hours. Change the location and direction of the seat or swing. Looking at the same 10 feet of room could get very tiresome. Remember that variety is as important to children as it is to adults. Change your baby's position in her crib during her waking hours—she will probably develop a sleeping position that she prefers (tummy down is suggested while sleeping so that the baby won't spit up and choke). Change the objects around her crib frequently; pastel sheets, a ceiling and the same mobile can get boring. If you could put yourself in her place, you could see just how much visual perception is increased by a changed environment. Even a slight turn of an infant seat opens up whole new vistas.

A wise and ancient custom is currently being revived that

greatly expands the not-yet-mobile child's environment. Many parents today are copying the Indian's method of carrying their children in a papooselike front- or backpack. The children feel warm, comforted, and secure. They also have the advantage of seeing so much more of the world than they would from a stationary position.

A wide variety of packs are available. A homemade one is easy to construct. It should have cushioned shoulder straps and a way of supporting most of your child's weight at your waist rather than on your shoulders. It can be very comfortable. You can get your work done and still be in constant touch with your child. The backpack also makes it quite easy to take the youngest family member on family outings. Meanwhile, her world is opening up wider to her. Place her in front of a window or patio door, and she has the whole, ever-changing out-of-doors to observe. At other times place her on a blanket on the floor or, on a warm, sunny day (use sunscreen), on a blanket in the yard. This idea of variety is so simple that it can be overlooked.

Enhance Strength and Coordination

As your child's strength and coordination develop, encourage her to reach out for objects. As you did with the rattle, place a toy just beyond her reach and she'll begin to roll, crawl, and eventually walk to get it. We do not mean to suggest that all of her toys should be beyond her reach. Offer your baby plenty of them to play with, but have a particularly inviting item just beyond reach. Keep her motivated to move and stretch.

Also encourage your baby to reach out with her feet. Suspend a sturdy plush toy near her feet. Let her kick it and observe its movements when she does. Keep it high enough not to entangle her feet. Again, bring in new objects so your infant's toes can feel different surfaces and textures. She is finding newfound strength with her developing legs. Encourage her to use them. (*Note:* Use this activity with an infant of age 5 months or less.)

Enabling Your Curious Toddler to Explore

Even before your child reaches the toddler stage, she becomes independently mobile by crawling. You must keep low cupboards filled only with items with which she can safely play. In the bathroom, towels and bathtub toys are safe for your child to get into; in the kitchen, pots and pans and plastic bowls are safe. Store dangerous items like cleansers, cleaners, polishes, and soaps in high and/or locked spots that are inaccessible to your child's exploring fingers. Remember, window cleaner looks obviously nonconsumable to you, but to your child it may look like an inviting drink of blue or purple fruit juice. Even dish detergent is hazardous if taken internally. The time to childproof your home is *before* your child reaches this independent stage of locomotion. Read the labels of household products before your child begins to crawl, and lock away all such objects.

Now that she is mobile and exploring on her own, give her some freedom. Put away that antique vase for a year or two, or, if your house is large enough, teach her which areas she is free to explore and which she must avoid. Children learn quickly to discriminate between permissible areas and off-limit ones.

Limit Restrictions and Recognize Skills

Parents should generally avoid using restrictive devices such as gates and playpens. Restricting a child does keep wear and tear on your house to a minimum, but allowing her freedom to climb and explore is much more beneficial than restricting her. Many children are raised in multilevel homes. In a multilevel home, give your child freedom time on the lowest level.

When she is mobile, begin training in climbing stairs. You can tell the developmental age of your child by how she manages stairs. It may sound simplistic to discuss mastering stairs; yet, when you see a first grader who leads with the one, same foot on every stair rather than alternating feet, you recognize that some rudimentary skills are not yet in place. When you notice that your child is getting curious about stairs, take time to show her how to master them. She will first learn to go up and down on her hands and knees. Then she will place both feet on each tread. Finally she will walk up and down with one foot after the other, as an adult naturally does. She will have a minor accident or two, but these usually occur after she has mastered the stairs rather than when she is just beginning. One stairway that does need modification is the one leading to a cement-floored basement. Place a thick rug or a beanbag chair over the cement at the bottom when your child is first learning to climb stairs.

Allow your child to be curious. Protect her from the house and protect the house from her, then let her explore.

Develop Small-Muscle Activities

Your home is literally filled with inexpensive objects that will be excellent learning tools for your child; for example, a baking dish filled halfway with dry cereal. When your child is older, you may also use varieties of uncooked pasta or beans, but be certain she is old enough to understand not to insert them into bodily openings (nose, mouth, ears). Add a few spoons and measuring cups, and your curious child will naturally explore. She will spend hours learning about pouring, relative sizes, textures, quantity, and so on. She'll probably make a mess, so confine this type of activity to an area that is easily cleaned.

Water play also provides many delightful learning minutes. Teach your child that many household objects (small toys, marbles, screws, balloons, etc.) can cause choking. Even some foods can be hazardous because her chewing and swallowing abilities are not fully developed. Therefore, she should avoid hard foods or large pieces of soft foods. Keep small objects out of reach and teach her not to laugh, play, or talk while eating. Your home is filled with numerous childproof, inexpensive (or free) pouring containers and other objects. Allow your child to pour water in outdoor settings or in sinks and the bathtub. Time for water play is especially appealing on days (or hours of the day) when your child is fretful. Another good pouring experience comes from an outdoor sandbox or an indoor sand table. Add an inexpensive toy car or truck, and she will play and learn by doing. If you like less mess for an indoor sand table, consider filling it with whole grain rice (uncooked, of course). Each time you add a new article to the play area (and remove one, if it's getting crowded), the learning takes on a whole new dimension. Watch for the unusual—a free, transparent plastic tube designed for paper towels becomes a source of much delight when rice is funneled through it.

Some parents cringe at the thought of finger paints. To avoid too much of a mess, add a bit of food coloring to liquid soap and let your child finger paint on the sides of the bathtub. There will be no messy clothes, and whatever mess she does create washes right down the drain.

"Babies create clutter. It is as natural as breathing. A cluttered house with a 10-month-old baby is, all other things being equal, a good sign. In fact, an immaculately picked-up house and a 10-month-old baby who is developing well are, in my opinion, usually incompatible" (p. 101). These words of Dr. Burton L. White (1987), an expert on early childhood, help comfort parents as their children go through the intensely curious stage of childhood. Although creating some clutter is natural, young children can learn to put things away. A miniature broom and dustpan are fun for the child who enjoys modeling after her mom and dad.

Your 2-year-old can help put cans on shelves when unloading groceries. At this age, the *idea* of helping rather than the actual amount of work done is the important thing. She should be verbally rewarded for helping even though you could do the job easier alone. In the long run, your child will establish habits of tidiness. Do *not* sacrifice her intellectual growth, her explosive curiosity, and her explorations of her world for the sake of a perfectly picked-up house. Allow your child to move and explore.

Sharing Movement Activities Outside the Home

Expand your child's explorations beyond the limits of your home. Continuing your role as guide and teacher, find new areas for her to explore.

Explore Nature Together

Take her on walks and point out nature's changes. For example, show her water changing to ice in winter and changing back to water in the spring on a lake you pass every day. Explore an icy puddle on a frosty morning and return to it at noon as its liquid glistens in the midday sun. These are among the simplest of lessons, but they will fascinate the youngest observer.

Continue this exploration of the effects of temperature on water by bringing a dish of ice or snow into your home. Watch what happens to it indoors. Read your child a story that relates to her new experience: *The Snowy Day*, by Ezra Jackson Keats (1962), tells of a boy who brings a snowball into his home in his pocket, forgets that it is there, and later wonders where it went. You can follow up on your real-life experience later in the day with a snow song or an art project with a snow theme. For example, make a snow scene using "snow" made by mixing soap flakes and water with a hand beater. In these ways your child's physical explorations carry over quite naturally into her language, artistic, and intellectual development. Remember, you are raising the whole child, not just the sum of her parts.

Just try looking at the world through her eyes, and the variety of exploration possibilities becomes almost limitless. Jean Piaget, renowned Swiss psychologist, stressed the importance of linking physical, sensory actions in the development of the thought

136, 182

College of St. Francis Library
Joliet, Illinois

processes of children. Piaget provides a comprehensive account of how the child develops intelligence, how the child comes to know objects and then begins to group events and ideas in the surrounding world (Sutton-Smith, 1973).

Piaget divides intellectual development into two major periods. The first period, sensorimotor, extends from birth to almost 2 years and the dominant emphasis is on overt physical action. The infant is busy with physical acts (sucking, sitting, walking) through which intelligence is derived. The second major period, conceptual, begins at about 18 months and extends to 15 years of age. The first major stage of the conceptual period is the preoperational stage, which extends from 18 months to 7 years. Language emerges and becomes sophisticated as concepts develop through concrete explorations (real experiences that involve the senses and physical activity). The ancient Chinese proverb, "What we hear, we forget; what we see, we remember; but what we do, we understand," applies to the way children learn.

Watch Television Together

Actual experience is so much more meaningful than the pseudo-experience that even the finest television program offers. When you do find an especially good program that you'd like your child to watch, though, watch it with her! Studies have shown that the child who watches an educational program with an adult and verbally interacts with the adult about it learns much more than the child who watches the same program alone. Remember, it is too easy to let the television set babysit so that you can attend to other matters. Instead, try to control the quality and quantity of your child's television viewing, and watch *with* her.

Visit Community Sites Together

Further expansion of your child's environment can occur when you go beyond your neighborhood. Don't hesitate to take your very young explorer to zoos, museums, farms, factories, and so on. Remember, however, that her attention span is short, and the outing is primarily her experience, not just yours. Expose her to as many different positive experiences as you can. A walk through the zoo can be filled with wonder if only you look at it through her eyes. Even if she is attracted to a crack on the sidewalk, stop to look at it and discover the possible reasons for its existence. This requires your time, but what better gift can you

College of St. Francis Library
Joliet, Illinois

give your child than yourself? None! Rejoice that she has the capability of wondering. Many cities provide listings of events or places that are of special interest to children. Check a newspaper or call city hall, the park department, or the library.

Broadening Your Child's Social Influences

Your child has come a long way in her ever-expanding world. She has progressed from a womb to a room to a home to a neighborhood and now to the universe. Can you continue to let her grow? Yes, simply by expanding the number of people whose viewpoints she is exposed to. In the beginning it was mostly Mom, but soon Dad and immediate family were included. Eventually, neighbors, relatives, and playmates began to influence your child's perceptions. Encourage this step-by-step progress, for it leads to our ultimate goal in child-rearing: a happy, well-adjusted, creative adult. You were her first and most influential teacher, but you must not try to shelter her from other influences. Other people must be allowed to guide and nurture her so she can see the world not only through your eyes but through the eyes of the universe.

Research-Established Preschool Options

One of these outside influences could be an established preschool. Many types of nurseries and preschools are available. When deciding which to select, use as much care as you do when making any other major decision. When you buy a home or a car, you shop around a lot to find the best quality for the best price. You might even consult a consumer's guide or another resource to assist you in your choice. Isn't your child one of the most important investments of your life? Shouldn't you spend at least an equal amount of time selecting a preschool, which will be molding your child's thoughts and ideas?

Check your local preschool alternatives. Some schools are church-affiliated, some are privately owned, and some are franchised operations. Frequently, libraries offer classes for preschool children. Day-care centers are becoming more available to the working mother. YMCAs and YWCAs offer nursery school programs, day care, and specialized classes according to age. All of these options merit your consideration, so investigate each one.

The YMCA offers a unique preschool program that addresses the development of the whole child. The Gym-n-Swim class, led by a qualified movement exploration teacher, encourages children to develop to their fullest potential by incorporating mind, body, and spirit in every activity. For example, your child may be given a ball and asked how many ways she can make it move and how many ways she can throw it. A good movement education teacher delights in the ideas that her properly inspired pupils suggest. Preschool classes in most YMCAs involve the parents learning *with* their child; however, many 4- and 5-year-olds enjoy short classes without Mom or Dad.

Some children, however, are apprehensive about classes. This apprehension may reflect their parents' own misgivings or reluctance to let go. Therefore, when taking your child to any preschool class for the first time, remember that she senses what you are feeling. Help her off to a good start by feeling confident, happy, curious, and eager to experience a new situation; most likely she will, too.

Last but certainly not least, remember the excellent experiences that are offered at most local churches or synagogues. Religious-school teachers and activities are often interesting, creative, and thought provoking. Furthermore, when you become involved as a volunteer, both of you learn and experience more.

Organize a Neighborhood Preschool Group

Another option for expanding the number of qualified people who work with your child is to organize your own neighborhood preschool group. Have each mother or father whose child belongs to the group assume responsibility for the group on a rotating basis. The group can meet 3 to 5 days a week; choose the hours that best suit your group.

To have a successful group, every parent must contribute time and effort. On your day to have the group, do whatever you enjoy doing the most—the children will enjoy it, too. One parent may enjoy parks and walks, so may treat the group to a picnic in the park. Another may be an expert baker, so may supervise as the children bake simple cookies or cakes. Another may be musically or artistically talented, so the group could sing, experiment with musical instruments, or try an art project. Do what you are comfortable doing, and you will find yourself enjoying your time with the group as much as the children do.

There are several advantages of developing your own preschool group:

- Less expense than other programs

- More opportunity for you to interact with your child
- More flexibility than a structured program.

There are also disadvantages, however. Because the leadership is not professional, some parents may not follow through with their responsibilities. Also, the "curriculum" may be hit-and-miss rather than sequentially and professionally organized.

Consider Preschool Options Carefully

Whichever you choose—a neighborhood play group, a formal nursery school, a YMCA or YWCA class, a library session, or a combination of these options—take time in making your selection.

- Find out the philosophy behind each program.
- Find out what equipment is available for your child's use.
- Visit the class a few times before making a decision.
- Listen to the teacher's questions and observe her reactions to various situations. Will she have a positive influence on your child?
- Take the time to find out and consider the advantages and disadvantages of the various options.

If you are contemplating the purchase of a new home, let the caliber of the schools your child will be attending help influence your decision. Find out whether your child's growth will be enhanced or hindered in her new environment. You can do this simply by observing classes at the school. Is there a spirit of friendliness and openness that would encourage your child's learning process? After you have made your choice and she is attending, give her a few weeks to adjust to the idea of being away from you; let her become established. Then call the school and ask when you may visit. Most schools welcome parents.

Stay Involved!

Be open to different methods of teaching, but ask yourself some of the following questions:

- Does the teacher encourage exploration while remaining mindful that certain basic facts must be mastered to facilitate this exploration?
- Is the teacher flexible enough to allow some creativity, yet

firm enough to channel that creativity into meaningful learning experiences?

- Are things well organized so that little time is wasted?
- Do the children enjoy working hard at school?

If you are happy about your child's progress, let the school administration and teacher know it. Praising the extra efforts of a really good teacher will encourage him or her to put out even greater effort. After all, everyone needs and thrives on positive reinforcers.

If the teaching techniques aren't as expansive as you'd like to see for your child, ask the teacher whether you could assist in the classroom. Perhaps the class is too large to teach more than the basics. Two recent studies found cutting class size in kindergarten to grade 3 improved self-image, social skills, attendance, and test scores (Morganfield, 1988). An extra pair of hands can make a great deal of difference in the classroom. Also, perhaps the PTA can assist in getting a truly inspiring speaker who can influence the school staff and even the district staff. Another suggestion might be to talk to the principal: Express your philosophy on child-rearing and ask whether your child could be placed with a teacher whose philosophy parallels yours.

Become involved in your local school board, where philosophy becomes school district policy. Many parents do not realize the capabilities they have for influencing the individual teacher, the principal, the school, and even the district staff. The teacher, the principal, the school, and the district that welcome constructive parental involvement are most receptive to new ideas. Those not receptive to parental involvement are probably too structured to accept new ideas.

Another way for parents, teachers, and children to be involved with each other is a joint project. The project could be devising math games that the children can play during the summer months or organizing a workshop to build a piece of equipment for classroom use, such as a puppet case for puppet shows.

Conferences should also mutually involve parents, teachers, and children. Results of classroom tests and teacher observations could be analyzed to point out strengths and weaknesses of the student; objectives could be set; methods of meeting these objectives could be established; and, in subsequent conferences, these objectives and results could be reevaluated and new objectives set. This cycle should be continual and should involve the parents, the teachers, and the children, which allows much more learning to occur. Children's horizons are expanded according to the number of new ideas to which they are exposed. Other people are helping to guide them through the wonders of the universe.

Developing Fitness for Fun

As your child seeks to expand her horizons, she needs basic guidelines that will lead her to a healthy and productive adulthood. Parents and teachers try to instill in children habits of cleanliness, such as washing before eating, using the toilet, keeping their bodies clean, and brushing their teeth.

However, modern education often neglects to provide daily exercise periods. Exercise should become as much a daily habit as brushing teeth or washing hands. Regular physical activity should begin in earliest infancy so it becomes established as a natural part of a daily routine. If it is not started until elementary school physical education classes, it will not become a natural part of living. Rather, it might become just part of a school curriculum that doesn't have much relevance to real life.

Make Activity a Daily Habit

How many of you have attended a class but discontinued the activity as soon as the class was completed? Physical activity should not be similarly temporary; it should have become a daily habit long before your child ever entered school. From reading the numerous studies that prove the benefits of exercise, educators recognize the need for daily exercise and require that approximately 150 minutes per week be spent in physical education. Parents also need to recognize these benefits. Would you wait until your child was 6 years old to teach her to brush her teeth, bathe, or use the toilet? Today's world, full of labor-saving conveniences, does not demand much physical exertion, so parents must instill the habit of daily physical activity in their children just as they instill such basic good health habits as brushing teeth.

Countless research studies show that exercise improves the cardiovascular system, decreases the risk of heart attack, improves muscle tone, increases the feeling of well-being, and improves the energy level. Even bees in a space shuttle experiment demonstrably suffered from the results of inactivity: Atrophy and eventual death occurred. When volumes of studies prove the benefits of exercise, how can parents not foster it in young children so that it becomes a lifelong habit?

Moderate exercise can be especially beneficial for children who have chronic illness, such as diabetes, epilepsy, or lung disease. Dr. Paul Stephens and his associates (1988) say that exercise improves disease control for some of these children, and, as for all children, exercise improves physical and mental fitness, encourages normal social and psychological development, and ultimately reduces the risk of cardiovascular disease. Consult your doctor for any special directions for a child with chronic disease; for example, salt intake and good hydration are especially important for a child with cystic fibrosis. Furthermore, physicians can offer suggestions for recognizing symptoms, such as those of hypoglycemia in a young diabetic athlete, as well as specific exercise suggestions, such as having a source of glucose (e.g., orange juice) available during and after exercise for a diabetic. Exercise is important for every child.

Ready, Set, Go!

Being fit for fun is simple. Start with your infant. From birth to 6 months, several minutes of playful cuddling will help establish a pattern of activity. From 6 months to 3 years, movement exploration activities provided by the parent will continue this pattern and develop into a special time for parent and child to move actively together. Set aside a definite time each day to move with your child, 10 minutes is usually long enough for the infant. Some families schedule their activity just before bath time. Use a clock so that you don't tend to rush your special time together. Remember, you are fostering behavior that will last a lifetime.

Both you and your child should dress in comfortable clothes; in a warm room, diapers should be sufficient for your child. Choose a warm but not hot area that has plenty of room for movement. Music adds to the fun during exercise and helps your child enjoy rhythm. Make it a fun time. Enjoy yourselves. Talk with your child about what you are doing and the feelings you are experiencing. Remember that her language and mental abilities develop right along with her physical prowess.

Chart her progress. Keep a record of the month she begins to sit up, crawl, climb shairs, walk, run, and so on. This information can be of value in her school years to her teachers, being helpful in unlocking styles of learning that best suit your child in her elementary years. Baby books aren't just for remembering the "good old days"—they can be a valuable tool for a teacher who understands child development. So often mothers are conscientious about recording the information about development for the first child, but they get "too busy" to be as conscientious with subsequent children. Later children should have as much attention to detail as that first child.

Moving Toward Optimal Health

The choice is yours.

Social regulations, modern transportation, television, schools, and other factors exert their influence on children to sit still. Yet, children's natural inclination is to learn by movement and exploration. Society must keep the social graces, the automobile, the TVs, and the schools. However, parents need to moderate such influence with alternatives such as the following:

- Encourage mobility and exploration around the house;
- limit the amounts of television watched (and video games played, too);
- join nursery schools or play groups that encourage inquisitiveness;
- get involved in your local schools; and
- make the enjoyment of an activity period as much a part of your whole family's daily life as brushing teeth.

To help you and your child get moving toward optimal health, numerous movement exploration activities are offered in chapter 4. As you read the previous three chapters, you noted that there are definite stages of development in these formative years. You will find that the exercises are designed to reflect the needs and capabilities of these varied stages. Look ahead to find activities that are designed to maximize your child's wellness whether she is an infant, a toddler, a preschooler.

Chapter 4

Movement Exploration Activities for Parents and Children

The benefits of participating in regular exercise are well documented and include such positive effects as improved cardiovascular and pulmonary systems; stress reduction; improved muscle tone, strength, endurance, and coordination; and an overall feeling of well-being. These are only a few of the known benefits of exercise, and they apply to children as well as adults. Habits begun in childhood affect later health patterns in either a positive or a detrimental way.

Normally infants wave their arms and legs and change their body positions. It is natural for babies to kick and reach out. If this natural activity could be channeled into an enjoyable, structured part of each day from infancy onward, then a lifelong movement habit would be developed. As you introduce a daily fitness ingredient into your child's lifestyle, you are also developing a daily exercise habit for yourself, so these physical activities and this exercise time are for you, too. Enjoy them!

Some general exercise principles and considerations need to be presented before the actual activities. The infant 6 months and older moves through warm-up and gentle stretching. Toddlers also use warm-up and stretching movements, but the activities can become a little more complex and organized. The preschooler builds on the previous movements and adds the new dimension of aerobic exercise, such as in running, jumping, and swimming (when available).

The physical activities are presented by listing the purpose of each, the equipment needed, and a description or explanation of how the movement is performed, including any precautions or limitations. Although the purpose of every activity is to improve physical development, it is equally important that you and your child are learning, creating, having fun, and enjoying the movement together. Although this point is extremely pertinent to each activity, it will not always be repeated.

Movement Guidelines and Suggestions

Starting with a few guidelines will make activity times more beneficial and fun for you and your child.

- Do only those activities that are suited to your child's age and development. For example, head-turning activities are encouraged for a 4-month-old, but you should wait until head muscle control is strong before attempting activities such as the "Pull-Up." Be gentle in moving your child; never force the movement, but encourage it instead. A good rule in all stretching is that it be gently done, rather than using force. Consult your general practitioner, pediatrician, or orthopedic doctor if you notice any possible problem, such as "toeing-in" of the feet.
- Be consistent. Set a time to move together and do it each day at the same time. Three or more days of active movement per week is a good habit to establish at an early age.

- Have a large movement space with a comfortable, soft surface, such as an exercise mat, a carpet, or a comforter.
- Keep the room temperature warm and pleasant.
- Wear minimal exercise clothing. It should be loose and comfortable to allow you to perspire naturally.
- Have aids such as a clock, music, pictures, a progress chart (for older children), and any equipment that is needed for particular activities.
- Make moving fun. You yourself must enjoy this time and activity because your child quickly senses your true feelings.

Movement Exploration for Infants

These activities are designed for fun and development. Your infant will delight in them, even though his mobility really depends on you.

Activity 1. Superman/Wonder Woman Chest

Purpose: To expand the chest and lungs and to promote shoulder flexibility.

Equipment: None.

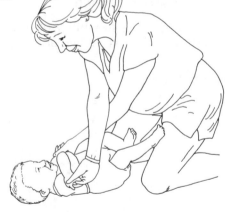

Description: Your baby is lying on his back. Let his fingers wrap around your forefingers. Gently stretch his arms out wide and then bring them back across his chest, expanding, then squeezing, his chest. Verbalize, "Out and in." Count off from 1 to 4 as you do the movement. You will be teaching him numbers and counting as well as positional words. Repeat four times.

Activity 2. Bicycle

Purpose: To move the hip and thigh muscles and to have fun in movement.

Equipment: None.

Description: Your baby is on his back. Grasp one of his calves and gently lift it up, bending the knee. At the same time, stretch the other leg down and somewhat straight as if he were bicycling or pumping. Do in sets of 4, counting "1, 2, 3, 4," then let him kick freely. Repeat 4 times. Don't jerk the legs.

Activity 3. Hamstring Stretch

Purpose: To increase flexibility of the back and of the hamstrings (if these are not stretched properly, back problems could result).

Equipment: None.

Description: With your baby lying on his back, place your thumbs against his calves and your fingers over his knees, keeping the knees relatively straight. Bring his feet slowly and gently toward his head. Gradually stretch farther over the course of many days and weeks. Do not force the movement or attempt to move beyond the normal range of motion; keep his shoulders on the floor. Verbalize, "Up and down." Repeat 3 or 4 times.

Activity 4. Bottom's Up

Purpose: To promote flexibility of the back.
Equipment: None.

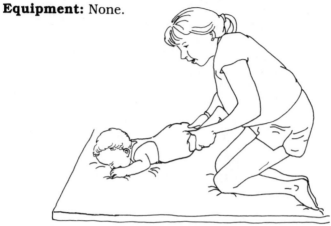

Description: Your baby is on his abdomen on the mat. Slip your hands under his thighs and lift up gently so that his hips are slightly hyperextended. Verbalize, "Up and down." Repeat 4 or 5 times. After a few months your baby will try to arch his back. Later remove your hands; your baby's legs will come up for the beginnings of an arch.

Activity 5. Double Leg Stretch

Purpose: To stretch the anterior leg muscles.
Equipment: None.

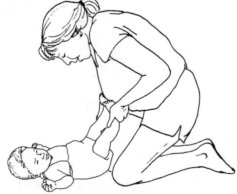

Description: Your baby is on his back. Face him while you are on your knees. Grasp his heels. Lift gently upward as you slightly straighten his knees. Repeat 5 times; gradually increase this number as time goes on.

Activity 6. The Grip

Purpose To strengthen the grip and arms.
Equipment: None.

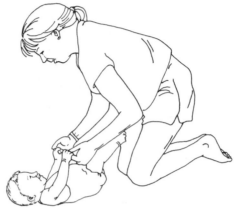

Description: Your baby is lying on his back. You are on your knees, facing your child. Let his fingers wrap around your forefingers. Draw his hands and arms toward you.

Activity 7. Ankle Rotation

Purpose: To strengthen feet and ankles.
Equipment: None.

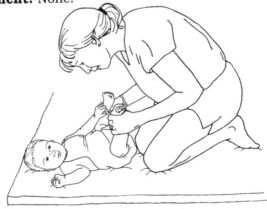

Description: Place your baby on his back on the mat. Place the soles of his feet together—gently, as always. Then turn his toes outward. Next, doing one foot at a time, gently rotate his foot outward and back at the ankle. Repeat with the other foot. (If your child has any lower extremity problems, first check with your physician.) Repeat 4 times with each foot.

Activity 8. Flying Spaceship

Purpose: To strengthen back muscles, chest muscles, balance, and the parent's abdominal muscles.
Equipment: None.

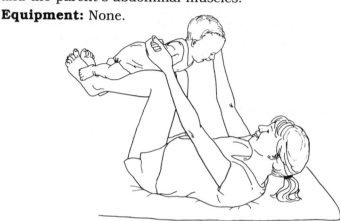

Description: You sit with your knees bent; your baby leans against your lower legs, facing you. He holds your thumbs while you grasp his hands. You slowly lean backward while bringing your knees up and feet—and baby—off the floor until you've rolled back onto the mat. Spread your baby's arms outward like the wings of an airplane to slightly extend his arch. Verbalize, "Down, up" and "out, in." Then slowly return to the sitting position.

Activity 9. Wooden Spoon Pull-Up

Purpose: Strengthen the grip and arms.
Equipment: Wooden kitchen spoon.

Description: Your older infant is on his back. Present a wooden spoon so that he grips it with both hands. Place your thumbs gently over his fingers to keep them in place (the need for this step will diminish as he gains strength). Then simply raise and lower his arms. Verbalize, "Up, down." Later, when his grip and neck are stronger, you can actually raise him slightly off the floor. This simple movement can continue into early childhood by your simply replacing the spoon with a wooden dowel or a broom handle.

Activity 10. The Elevator

Purpose: To strengthen the neck and back and the parent's arms.

Equipment: None.

Description: While you are lying on your back, lay your older infant face-down on top of you. Hold him by his waist and raise him *slowly* up so that he is at arm's length above you. Then lower him. Verbalize, "Up and down," and count how many repetitions you can make. Start with 5 repetitions and increase 3 or 4 per week until you can do 25. Your baby will keep his body straight, strengthening his buttocks, his back, and his neck.

Moving With Your Toddler

Whereas your infant delighted you with his movements even though he could not walk, your toddler will never stop amazing you with what he can physically accomplish. In fact, now that he is mobile, one of your challenges is to hold his attention long enough to stick with your plan of a consistent activity period.

Therefore, plan ahead what you will do during that short but fun-packed period. Keep it short, perhaps 10 to 15 minutes long. Vary it according to your and your child's individual needs and interests. As you did when he was an infant, have a repertoire of activities to choose from so that his interest will be maintained. Again, be sure to talk him through each activity. Remember, you are helping the whole child develop.

The infant was not able to hold onto many things, but you will find that the use of simple equipment enhances movement at the toddler stage, although there are still several activities that can be done without equipment. In fact, many of the infant activities can be modified for the toddler. Now get ready to be fit for fun and to explore movement with your toddler.

Toddler Activities

These movement exploration activities are designed to encourage your toddler to gain confidence in his increasing mobility.

Activity 1. Arm Circles

Purpose: To warm up and stretch.
Equipment: None.

Description: You and your toddler stand with your arms outstretched sideways. Pretend the ends of your hands can draw shapes in the air. Use your hands to draw small circles in the air. Use your hands to draw big circles in the air. Ask your toddler whether he can make the circles go in the other direction. Ask him, "What other shapes can we make if we pretend our arms are giant paint brushes?" Also pretend that your arms represent airplane propellers, Dutch windmills, baseball pitchers' arms, or helicopter rotors. Encourage your toddler to also use the rest of his body in imitating, for example, an airplane starting, taking off, and flying. Keep the movement slow, rhythmical, and smooth.

Activity 2. High Low

Purpose: To warm up and stretch.
Equipment: None.

Description: You and your toddler stand on the mat. "Reach up toward the sky. Reach down toward the ground. Reach to touch a cloud. Reach down and see what you have found

[toes]." Reach *high* and reach *low*. Reach up to a high shelf for an imaginary box and put it next to your feet. Reach up to "pick an apple" and down to "put it in a basket." While doing this, don't lock your knees, and avoid bouncing. Repeat, then go to the next activity.

Activity 3. Headstrong

Purpose: To warm up.
Equipment: None.

Description: You and your toddler stand on a mat, feet apart for balance. "Show me a way you can move your head. Can you think of another way to make it move?" Continue until the child stops coming up with new ideas. Some ways for you to demonstrate until he gets the idea are side to side and front to back. Gentleness is the key with head and neck movements. Do not strain the vertebrae by doing head circles.

Activity 4. Lift Your Legs

Purpose: To warm up and to develop abdominal and back muscles.
Equipment: None.

Description: You and your toddler lie on your sides on the mat. "How can we lift our legs toward the sky? One leg? Other leg? Two legs? Can we find a different way to lie down and still get our legs up?" Lie on your back and raise one leg, then try the other leg.

Activity 5. The Cradle

Purpose: To build abdominal strength.
Equipment: None.

Description: Your toddler lies on his back with his knees to his chest and his arms around his knees. He slowly rocks back and forth and lets go of his knees, continuing to rock in a half-tuck position.

Activity 6. Creepy Crawler

Purpose: To develop coordination of the large muscles and cross-laterality.

Equipment: None.

Description: "Now that you are walking around, let's not forget about how we used to crawl. Crawling was good for our muscles; it is still good for us. Remember that the right leg moves when the left arm moves? We can crawl forward. We can crawl backward. What animals crawl like this? Let's pretend we are _____." Your crawling can be accompanied by vocalizations and characteristic actions associated with the animals, or appropriate recorded music.

Activity 7. Bunny Hopping

Purpose: To develop strength and coordination of the large muscles in the thighs and calves.

Equipment: None.

Description: "Let's pretend to be bunnies. Can you bend your body to look like a bunny? Can you move like a bunny? What you did is called 'hopping.' Can you hop again? Let's hop together. Now can you hop on one foot? Can you try the other one? Now let's stop hopping and bend over and nibble a carrot." Have a carrot ready and really eat it at the end of the activity. Make sure the carrot is finished before going on to a new activity.

Activity 8. Fun With Feathers

Purpose: To develop graceful movement.
Equipment: A feather and relaxing music.

Description: Hold up the feather and ask "What is this? What color is it? What can it do? [Float.] How can we make it go up? [Blow on it or throw it.] When it is up, does it stay up? How does it move when it is coming down? Let's turn on some soft music and pretend we are feathers that are turning and twisting softly toward the ground." Repeat by letting a "breeze" come along and blow you up to the sky again.

Activity 9. Balls Are Beautiful

Purpose: To develop hand-eye coordination and rolling, bouncing, and catching a ball.

Equipment: A soft, small ball (the best for catching are foam or cloth) about 4 to 6 inches in diameter. Some balls for the earliest little catchers and throwers have indented areas to make grasping easier. Larger rubber balls (8 to 12 inches) are best for bouncing. Have a variety of balls available.

Description: Balls are used in many diverse activities. Every activity should not be attempted on each single day, but some kind of ball handling should be part of the activity period from the earliest ages onward. These are just a few of the activities you can try.

- *Rolling the Ball.* You and your toddler sit facing each other, legs stretched out in Vs, feet about 3 feet apart. Ask your child, "How can I get this ball over to you? I can push it like this. This is called 'rolling the ball.' Can you roll it back to me?" Notice that your toddler is always expanding his vocabulary as he grows physically. Even if he is not saying the words back to you, he is still absorbing what you say. Continue this activity for as long as his interest holds. On the next day, roll the ball again and use the words again, but then try some of the following ball activities for diversity.
- *Let the Ball Fall.* Standing on a hard-surfaced area, you with one ball and your toddler with a different one, verbalize,

"Can you let your ball go? What happens to it? [It falls to the floor.] What happens when this kind of ball falls to the floor? [Rubber ball bounces back up toward thrower.] How are these balls the same? How are they different? [Colors, compositions, etc., differ]. Which do you like better? Which do you play with? You try dropping the ball and see what happens." Much later, after much experimenting he can be encouraged to try to catch the ball, but this comes only after lots of experimenting on letting it go."

- *Catching the ball.* "If we can get the ball back in our hands, it is called 'catching the ball.' What is it called? Let's see whether we can catch the ball. Good job!" Be sure to give lots of positive rewards with your words and tender touches when he does or says something well. Try this activity for several sessions.

- *Bouncing the ball.* "Now that we can catch the ball, can we try to give it a little pat? Let the ball go and when it comes back up to you, give it a little love tap. Good. That is called 'bouncing the ball.' Can you give it one bounce? What is it called? Can you make it bounce two times in a row?" Try this on into early childhood.

As your toddler's skill with balls continues to grow, keep practicing the basic skills of rolling, dropping, bouncing, and catching balls. Add more complex ball skills as your child is ready to try them. It is hard to say at what age this skill will occur, because it varies greatly from one child to another. The important thing to remember is not to ask him to do more than he is physically ready to do. If he meets each step with success, it really doesn't matter exactly at what age it occurs. Small steps, positively accomplished, are the goal.

You might introduce more complex activities by saying "Can you bounce this ball inside this hula hoop? Can you bounce the ball with the hand that isn't your better hand? Can you throw the ball up into the air, let it bounce once, then catch it?" Other complex activities with balls will be discussed in subsequent sections.

Activity 10. Body Parts

Purpose: To warm-up, to recognize and name body parts, and to have fun while moving.
Equipment: None.

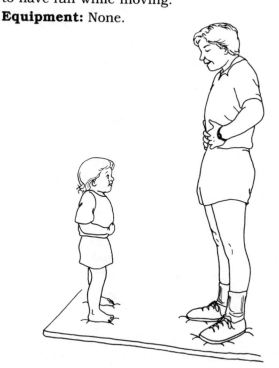

Description: You and your toddler stand on a mat, facing each other. "Let's play a guessing game. Can you touch what I touch? [Touch tummy.] This is my stomach. [Touch legs.] These are my legs. What are these? These are my arms. What are they? Can you touch your arms?" Continue this exercise every day, adding other body parts, including facial features. Always repeat the parts that are already part of your toddler's vocabulary before going on to teach a new one. Touch parts of the body that make your toddler stretch, twist, and reach.

As with the infant activities, use your imagination and ingenuity to create more and different movement experiences for your toddler. For example, with the addition of balls, dozens of activities can be developed. However, don't be too eager and start complex ball skills such as those used in volleyball, baseball, basketball, and so on. Keep the activities simple; let your child have success in simple skills before advancing to more difficult ones.

Additional equipment that will elicit ideas for movement exploration could include ropes, balloons, beanbags, slides, ladders, balance beams, and cardboard boxes. All of these give your toddler new ideas and activities to explore.

Preparing Your Preschooler to Be Fit for Fun

Toddlers are approximately 1 to 3 years of age. They progress from having just begun to walk to becoming coordinated enough to walk, run, and jump with relative ease, before reaching the preschool stage. Although the precise age varies from child to child, most children reach this skill level by the age of 3.

The preschool stage explodes with newfound skills—not only physical but also verbal, social, and intellectual. The good habits began when they were infants and took on new dimensions when they were toddlers. By the time they enter grade-school physical education programs, physical activity will already have been established as a natural part of their day.

Activity in the infancy stage was typified by warm-up movement. These same activities (or variations of them) were continued for toddlers, with the addition of exploratory movements. The preschool stage builds on these two cornerstones and adds a third dimension—vigorous activity that promotes good aerobic health.

Aerobic Exercise Guidelines for Preschoolers and Adults

Most programs for aerobic fitness have focused on adults. Although children are beginning to receive more attention, too often adult standards are imposed upon them. Program modifications are needed when considering preschoolers and aerobics. For example, consider resting heart rates. The normal resting heart rate for adults is 72 beats per minute. The normal heart rate for young children is quite different. Whaley and Wong (1979) give the following as normal rates.

- 120 beats per minute for 1- to 11-month-olds
- 110 beats per minute for 2-year-olds
- 100 beats per minute for 4- to 6-year-olds
- 90 beats per minute for 8-year-olds

As body mass and age increase, the heart rate decreases. Young children have higher heart rates quite naturally. Thus, aerobic definitions and requirements must be modified for young children. Adult aerobic activities are those requiring continuous activity for approximately 15 to 20 minutes. The heart rate should be between 60 percent (beginners) and 85 percent (maximum) of the age-adjusted maximum heart rate.

Note: 220 – age = maximum heart rate for adults.

Interval Training

Adults can also train aerobically by doing interval training. This is a system of physical conditioning in which the body is subjected to short, regularly repeated periods of work interspersed with periods of relief.

Children do a type of interval training on their own with little or no encouragement: If they see a butterfly, they spurt ahead to try to catch it. Older children will be ready to participate in sustained aerobic activities if they have been active as infants, toddlers, and preschoolers. Aerobic activities for adults are often sustained activities. However, preschoolers have difficulty keeping interest in sustained activities. Parents and educators realize that they are unlikely to maintain preschoolers' interest in strenuous activity. We believe that with the naturally faster heart rates of young children as well as their limited interest in sustained activities, the best way to introduce aerobics is by encouraging interval-training-type activities.

Explain Huff-and-Puff Activities

Aerobic activities can be explained to your preschooler in this way: "They are activities that make us huff and puff or breathe hard. When this is happening, our hearts are working extra hard to carry oxygen around to all the parts of our bodies. This is good for them because it exercises them and makes them stronger. It also exercises our lungs and blood systems [pulmonary and circulatory systems]. When these systems are strong, we are ready for anything that life has to offer. We can check whether our heart rates went up by feeling a 'beeping' called the *pulse*."

Let him feel his pulse both before exercising (at resting rate) and after exercising (at working rate). "Our pulse rates go up for many reasons. If we have been exercising, the rate goes back down to a slower rate quickly because our hearts are strong and can recover quickly." If possible, let him hear his heart through a stethoscope at the two different heart rate levels.

Your child will respond positively when encouraged to do interval-training activities that raise his heart rate or make him huff and puff. Our own children enjoyed being timed with a stopwatch and trying to beat their old time. Variety is the key factor in sustaining interest. One day we'd try a 50-yard run, the next a 50-yard skip or hop.

A game the children loved from earliest ages onward was simply called Chase. We chased each other around several of our own apartments and homes through the years. The fun can happen no matter what the weather is like outdoors. When our children were older, we sometimes added a spooky effect: We would surprise each other in dim light, then the chase would be on. Our best houses for this were ones that had a circle pattern (i.e., you could go from room to room to room in a full loop).

Activity Session Suggestions

The main ideas to remember in thinking of your young child and aerobics are these:

- He is not an adult, having a different heart rate, endurance level, attention span, and so on.
- He likes a variety of activities.
- He does interval training quite naturally if you give him the opportunity and encouragement.

Vigorous spontaneous activities in the preschool stage promote continued aerobic fitness in later childhood and adulthood.

Warm-Up

Your preschooler's exercise session should begin with some warm-up movements for every area of his body. Some of the warm-up activities from the infant and toddler sections can be used; in fact, these are actually the lead-up movements for adult warm-up exercises. The main difference with the preschooler's warm-up is that it is done more quickly and with briefer explanations.

Workout

The warm-up should be followed by a variety of exploratory and experimental movements that are relatively vigorous. The transition through the stages of development can be illustrated by observing how a balloon would be used in each of the three different stages. When you give a balloon to an infant, he feels it, rubs it, and pushes it. A toddler also does these things, but then he begins to see how it moves when he throws it up. The preschooler does all of the above but also uses a variety of body parts to keep it up in the air. It will never cease to amaze you how many different ways the preschooler can make himself and the balloon move.

If we watch a grade-school child using the same balloon, he naturally devises his own type of a game with it. Thus, you wouldn't be surprised to see an 8-year-old using a complex soccer kick. Compare him to the 5-year-old, who moves the balloon with his hands, elbows, arms, and feet while moving through space with fine coordination. The 2-year-old enjoys the balloon just as much, but he may just hold it while running, or he may stand still and throw it up into the air with two hands. Every child enjoys the same piece of equipment. However, with each successive stage, children move with more coordination and creativity. It is pure joy to observe the blossoming development of young children.

The preschooler's period of vigorous activity should include some type of interval or sustained aerobic activity, such as running, swimming, or bicycling. From earliest childhood, he needs to exercise his heart so that it becomes efficient enough to resist the degenerative process of heart disease.

Your preschooler might want to go walking or jogging with Mom or Dad. He sees the rest of the family enjoying activity, as part of their daily lives, so he wants to join in. A circular track (indoors or outdoors) works best for jogging with a young one. Some member of the family is always close to him to encourage him and watch out for his safety. Of course, the preschooler doesn't run continuously, as adults do. He can become distracted by a nearby flower or a rock near the track. That's all right. He's enjoying the activity period, and that is what's important—establishing good habits right from the start. Even when adults run, we observe the beauties of nature.

Never make running a chore. Ask your child (and yourself) to do only what can be done comfortably. Your 17-year-old can easily run with you for 5 miles around the lake. However, your 8-year-old is much happier biking that distance with you, and the 2-year-old won't be ready for that distance for several years.

The key to good health is to stay physically active, but don't exercise until it hurts. If it does, you are doing something that you are not enjoying—or that may be injuring you—and you will probably quit.

Your aim is no pain. The person who is really fit develops fitness gradually. While doing this, be sure to vary your activities. Intersperse aerobics, swimming, or biking with your jogging. Rather than exercising every day, give your muscles a rest at least 1 day a week. Working out 3 or 4 days a week is adequate. A Monday-Wednesday-Friday or a Tuesday-Thursday-Saturday sequence will allow you to enjoy exercising without overdoing it.

These fitness suggestions apply to both you and your child. Don't overdo it, progress gradually, vary the activities, and you and your child will be fit for fun.

Cool-Down

Your and your child's workout session consists of movement explorations followed by a period of vigorous activity, such as running, jumping, or swimming. This vigorous, aerobic period of the routine should be followed by a cool-down period. Due to exercise, blood is moving rapidly through the circulatory system; it needs a chance to slow down afterward without pooling in the lower body. An active cool-down allows this to happen. An experienced runner, for instance, walks after his run to allow him to safely return to his pre-exercise state.

Warm-Up Exercises for Your Preschooler

The following pages include some warm-up exercises, exploratory movements, and cool-down exercises for your preschooler.

Activity 1. Windmills (Alternating Toe Touches)

Purpose: To warm up.
Equipment: A picture of a windmill.

Description: You and your child stand on a mat, your feet apart. Show him a picture of a windmill. Talk about how the windmill rotates in the wind. Ask your child, "Can we make our arms stretch out? Can we make this arm reach down and touch the opposite toe? Can we reach the other arm down to touch the other toe?" Repeat 4 or 5 times.

Activity 2. Elephant Walk

Purpose: To warm up.
Equipment: A picture of an elephant.

Description: "Let's pretend that we are at the zoo. Do you know the name of this big animal? [Show the picture of an elephant.] That's right—it's an elephant. Show me how we could make our arms look like this part of the elephant. Do you know this part's name? That's right—it's his trunk. An elephant uses his trunk to pick up things. Let's pretend that we are elephants and that we have some things to pick up. Bend way over. Can you pick up that peanut? Let's do it again. Swing your trunk high!"

Activity 3. Row, Row, Row Your Boat

Purpose: To strengthen the grip and upper arms.
Equipment: None.

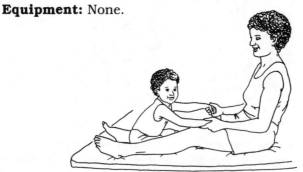

Description: You and your child sit facing each other on the mat. Spread your legs, your feet being outside your child's to accommodate the difference in leg lengths. Reach out and grab hands. Pretend you are rowing a boat, pulling a rope, or sawing wood. Gently rock back and forth with a gentle tugging motion. Increase the tension on the rocking motion as time goes by. Start with 5 back-and-forth motions; gradually increase this to 20 repetitions.

Activity 4. Tummy Tightener (Sit-ups)

Purpose: To warm up and to strengthen abdominal muscles.
Equipment: None.

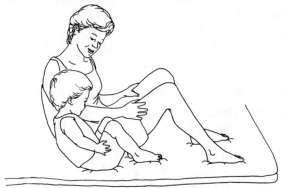

Description: "Do you remember what this part of your body is called? That's right, it's the abdomen. When you were little, we sometimes called it your *tummy*. Here's a way to help your tummy be strong like the rest of you. There are lots of important things inside here—like your stomach and intestines—but no bones to protect them. So we want our abdominal muscles not to be soft and squishy, but instead to be strong and firm and protective. Let's lie back. Now bend your knees. You can put your hands anywhere you want to be comfortable. [Beginners may place them on their thighs to help pull themselves up.] Now let's see whether we can sit up. Let's try a few more. That's enough for today." Remember, your young child's muscles cannot support a lot of repetitions. Very gradually work up to more repetitions.

Activity 5. Let's Be a Bridge

Purpose: To strengthen the muscles of the back, the buttocks, and the legs.
Equipment: None.

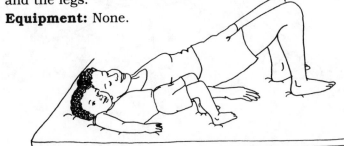

Description: You and your child lie on your backs with your hands at your sides. Both of you slowly raise your buttocks off the ground as high as possible until your weight is on your heels, hands, and shoulders. Hold this position for a count of 5. Gradually increase to a count of 20.

Activity 6. Scared Caterpillar

Purpose: To strengthen the abdominal muscles.
Equipment: None.

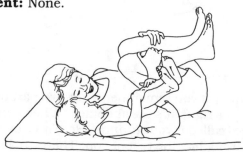

Description: You and your child lie on your backs. Slowly pull your knees up to your chests or as far as you can. Once they are up, grasp your legs and hold. Return to a lying position and repeat if possible. Work up to 10 repetitions.

Activity 7. Alligator (Push-Ups)

Purpose: To strengthen the back and arms.
Equipment: None.

Description: You and your child assume push-up positions, holding your body weight up with your hands and feet. Slowly walk forward, then backward, until the position can be held for 1 minute. Gradually advance to touching the chest (just the head, for beginners) to the floor and raising the back up again, resting between movements. Work up to 10 repetitions. Ask your child, "What kind of animal do we look like?"

Activity 8. Look Around the Mountain

Purpose: To strengthen the abdominal muscles.
Equipment: None.

Description: You and your child lie on your backs with your knees bent, your heels near your buttocks, and your hands at your sides. Slowly raise your heads and shoulders off the mat. Look at your toes on the left side. Move back to the starting position, then raise up again and look at your toes on the right side. Work up to 10 repetitions.

Activity 9. Be a Gorilla

Purpose. To strengthen the thighs and lower legs.
Equipment: None.

Description: You and your child assume apelike positions: your knees bent slightly, hands hanging at sides, and bodies slightly bent over. Move around the room in this position, gradually increasing the duration of this movement to 3 minutes.

Activity 10. He-Man Lift

Purpose: To strengthen the thighs, upper arms, and back.
Equipment: A 1-pound beanbag or soft weight.

Description: Place the bean bag or soft weight on the floor in front of your child. He picks up beanbag by bending at the knees and lifting it over his head like a weight lifter. He then places it back on the floor. Repeat 4 or 5 times, gradually working up to 20 repetitions.

Exploring Movement With Your Child

Movement exploration is your consciously allowing, even encouraging, your child to move in a variety of ways. Your child begins to explore how his own body can move and also how he can make a number of objects move in a limitless variety of ways.

Your preschooler should repeatedly perform each of the suggested variations of the following movement exploration activities. Accompany his efforts with much positive reinforcement. Have him do just two or three variations of each activity per day, slowly progressing as he develops and masters the movement skills. Accomplishing all the suggested variations—not to mention those of your own and his own creation—will take many months. We have included many ideas so you can use this book for a long time.

Movement Exercises

Activity 1. Balance Beam

Purpose: To improve balance and visual-motor control.

Equipment: A balance beam approximately 2 to 3 inches off the floor, or low enough that your child will approach it with confidence. This beam can be made from a 10-foot length of a two-by-six or four-by-six board. (*Note:* Earliest balancing can be done with the board directly on the floor to add confidence; the very young child has a natural awareness of height.)

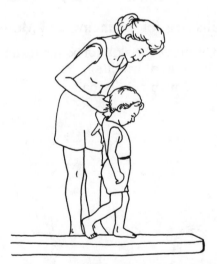

Description: "Can you walk slowly across the beam? Can you stand sideways and still cross it? Backwards? Can you walk forward, stop in the middle, balance on one foot like a stork, and then continue walking to the end? Can you walk across carrying this pole [a broom handle or dowel]? Can you walk across the beam, stop in the middle, pick up a beanbag, place it on top of your head, then walk to the end? [Remind him to bend from his knees, not from his waist, while stooping to pick it up.] Can you cross the beam if you have to go through this hula hoop? [Tape it to the beam.] Can you go across if I have set up this obstacle [a plastic pole supported by two cones]? Can you walk across, turn a half-turn at the middle, then walk the rest of the way backward? Can you walk across if you are balancing a beanbag on the back side of each of your hands? [His head should be erect and his shoulders back for good alignment.] Can you carry a ball to the middle, bounce it once and catch it, then continue walking across? Can you bounce and catch a ball after every four steps? Can you go to the middle and balance like a swan, bending forward at your waist, stretching out your arms and one foot for balance? Can you walk like a monkey across the beam? Like a cat? Can you catch this ball if I throw it to you while you are on the beam? Can you walk across with your eyes shut? Blindfolded?" Older children can advance with these same activities by trying them on an even higher beam.

Activity 2. Balls Are for Bouncing and More

Purpose: To improve the skills of bouncing and catching, tossing and catching, and dribbling.

Equipment: A 7-inch rubber ball.

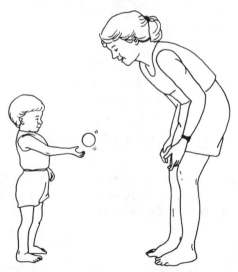

Description "Let the ball drop, then catch it. Give it a little push, as it drops, then catch it. Bounce and catch the ball. Use one hand, then two. Try the other hand. Which hand was easier? Bounce and catch it 5 times without dropping it. Then try for 10 times. Throw it lightly into the air and catch it. Do it 3 times without dropping it. Then do it 10 times. Bounce the ball, then clap once and catch it. Throw it over your head, let it bounce once, then turn around and catch it. Bounce it, then turn quickly and catch it before it falls again. Bounce it under your leg and catch it. Throw it up, then clap and catch it. See how many times you can clap before catching it. Toss the ball from one hand to the other like a juggler. Throw the ball into the air, then jump once and catch it. See how many times you can jump before you have to catch it. Try to hold the ball with your feet, your elbows, your knees. Jump like a rabbit while keeping the ball between your knees. Walk with the ball between your knees. Put the ball on the floor and jump over it forward and backward. Put the ball on the ground and see what parts of your body you can use to make it move. Bounce it between your knees and catch it. Hold it behind your head, let it bounce, and catch it with your hands backward. Bounce it several times in a row. Walk and bounce [dribble] it. Walk and dribble it way up high. Dribble it low. Dribble along a straight line on the floor. Dribble it between cones like a figure eight. Dribble slowly. Dribble fast. Try to dribble with each hand."

Activity 3. Hoop-De-Do

Purpose: To develop jumping skills, balancing skills, hopping skills, and recognition of body parts.

Equipment: A hula hoop.

Description: Place the hula hoop on the ground. "This is a hula hoop. What is it called? Can you stand inside the hoop? Outside? On the hula hoop? Go back inside the hoop. Can you find the center of the hoop? Can you stand near the edge? Are there any corners? Can you walk all along the edge of the hoop? What is its shape called? Go back to the center of the hoop. Can you balance on one foot while in the center? How long? How tall can you make yourself while balancing? Try the other foot. Can you balance on one foot and one hand? What other body part can you balance on? Can you tell me the name of that body part? Can you balance having two parts in the hoop and two parts outside the hoop? Can you change and put two different parts in and out? Can you jump up in the center of the hoop? How many times? Can you jump from the center to the outside? Back in again? Can you find another way to jump out of your hoop? How far can you jump out of your hoop and still be in control when you land? Can you jump with one foot in and one foot out? Can you hop on your right foot or on your left foot in the hoop?"

Activity 4. Rope a Winner

Purpose: To gain skill in walking patterns, jumping patterns, and hopping patterns.

Equipment: Two lengths of heavy (5/16-inch) rope. When one end of your child's rope is held to the ground by his foot, the other end reaches his armpits. Use this same method for determining the correct length for your rope.

Description: Tape the lengths of rope to the ground. Be barefoot. Ask your child, "Can you walk forward on top of the rope? Can you walk along the sides of the rope? Can you walk backward on top of the rope? Can you walk like a dog on your hands and knees, with the rope between your hands and knees? Can you do it on hands and feet? Can you hop over the rope with one foot? The other foot? Jump with both feet? Forward and backward? Can you walk sideways on the rope? Can you walk forward using a scissors walk? Can you jump down the length of your rope from one end to the other, each time landing on the other side? Can you hop all the way down on one foot? And on the way back, use your other foot? Can you find another way to get down the rope, keeping the rope between your legs?"

Activity 5. Bag Your Beans

Purpose: To develop throwing and catching skills.

Equipment: A beanbag. It is best to make it with your child so he can see what went in it. Use two four-by-four pieces of canvas filled with navy or pinto beans.

Description: "What is this bag called? What does it have inside? Can you throw it up into the air just a little way so that you can catch it without dropping it? Now how high can you throw it? How high can you throw it and still catch it? Can you throw it upward and catch it with just one hand? Can you throw it up, then catch it with the other hand? Can you throw it back and forth? How many times? Can you throw it up, then jump up to catch it? Can you throw it up, then clap and catch it? How many times can you clap? Can you pass it back and forth like a juggler? Can you put it on a body part, then flip it up and catch it? Try a different body part. Put the beanbag on your head. Can you walk with it up there? Put it on your head again and nod. Can you catch it as it falls off? Can you throw it up, then catch it with a body part other than your hands? Find other ways to toss and catch your bag of beans."

Cooling Down

When cooling down after vigorous activity, be sure to slow down from the rapid tempo of the music that you had selected for movement exploration. Then choose from any of the warm-up exercises previously listed. Other cool-downs could include the following:

Cool-Down Exercises for Your Preschooler

Activity 1. Lazy Lion

Purpose: To bring the heart rate down gradually after a vigorous aerobic period.

Equipment: None.

Description: Walk slowly (the best cool-down of all) for 1 or 2 minutes, occasionally reaching to the sky. Then walk on all fours like a "lazy lion."

Activity 2. Giant Step

Purpose: To stretch out the calf, leg, and thigh muscles.
Equipment: None.

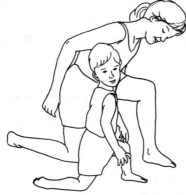

Description: "Let's take some big giant steps and then touch the knee of the back leg to the floor. Balance with your hands on each side of the forward knee. Stretch, don't bounce. Do 4 to 6 steps with each leg.

Activity 3. Cat Stretch

Purpose: To strengthen tnc lower back muscles.
Equipment: None.

Description: "Let's get down on our hands and knees and pretend we are cats. What does a cat say? Now pretend you have been a busy cat all day and now you are stretching and relaxing. Now keep your hands still but stretch your arms out. Reach way in front of you. Pretend you are a kitten that is pulling backward with his claws on the carpet. Kittens love to stretch. Let's stretch out again, pull on the floor, and come back."

Activity 4. Cat's Arched Back

Purpose: To strengthen the lower back muscles.
Equipment: None.

Description: "Let's pretend to be cats again. This time the cats are stretching their backs up toward the sky. Can you stretch your back up, and now relax? Let's do it again."

Activity 5. Imagine

Purpose: To totally relax all the muscles.
Equipment: None.

Description: You and your child lie on your backs on a mat with arms stretched over your heads. Say to your child, "Reach as far as you can with your hands and as far down with your toes. Take a deep breath and let your air out—don't force it out. Now slowly bring your arms over your head, closing your eyes as you bring your arms down to your sides. Imagine yourself at your favorite outdoor place, like a beach or a park. What place are you thinking about? It's a nice, warm, sunny day.

Keep your eyes closed. Take another deep breath as you exhale. Keep the outdoor picture in your mind, but also pretend you're light as a feather, just floating along. Take another deep breath and let it go. For 30 seconds I'm going to let you just think about your place and being light as a feather, starting now." At the end of the 30 seconds, slowly sit up and discuss how you felt.

Your preschooler is getting close to adult-type exercises and may want to try exercises done by Mom and Dad. Imagination, ingenuity, and variety are the key. Let him explore, experience, and experiment—and make sure he has fun.

A Few Tips About Adult Exercise

No chapter on exercise can be complete without a word about adult exercise habits. First of all remember, if you yourself don't exercise regularly, no amount of fitness teaching you give your child will be successful for long. However if he sees you interested in your own fitness activities, he will emulate you.

As your child matures, see what family activities you can do together. Some of his fondest memories of childhood will be of the softball games played with you or the daily family walk. By adding just one simple habit (taking a family walk around your neighborhood in the evening), not only can you take off 10 or more pounds in a year, but you also gain the closeness of a family activity that becomes a tradition. By the time your child is older, he will ask, "Is it time yet?" Taking a ball along and tossing it in a variety of ways just adds to the fun. Variety in the ball-tossing "rules" you create keeps the experience fun. Some examples: "You can catch it only if you are in front of Dad. You can try to catch it on one bounce." Letting him help create new rules keeps it fun.

Your exercise program can be coordinated with your child's, but his program will not be suitable for you. Many principles of good exercise do apply to adults just as they do to infants, toddlers, and preschoolers. However, these principles must be adapted and geared to the appropriate level, interest, attention span, and capabilities of the participant. Some of your child's activities, like the bunny hop, may be beyond the range of your flexibility or other abilities, so pace yourself. On the other hand, you may not be getting enough aerobic benefit and will need to find additional time for your own workout. There are books on adult fitness which have excellent, successfully tested guidelines.

Exercise Guidelines

The following basic exercise principles should have meaning both for you and for your children:

1. *Overload* principle states that you should progressively increase the intensity of the workouts over the course of the training program.
2. *Adaptation* follows overload. Adaptation is when the body adjusts to the level of work. Once adaptation occurs, overload is again applied and the cycle repeats itself.
3. *Frequency* refers to the number of times per week you exercise. The minimum number is 3 workouts per week, with a day between workouts.
4. *Duration* is the length of each exercise period. This should be between 45 and 60 minutes for adults, between 10 and 40 minutes for children, depending on their ages.
5. *Intensity* is the level at which you perform an activity. (Intensity in aerobic activities is defined as a percentage of maximum heart rate.) Working absolutely as hard as possible is thought of as maximum intensity. For example, if 10 push-ups is the maximum number that you can do, then 6 push-ups would be 60 percent of maximum. You should work between 60 and 80 percent of your maximum.
6. *Individual differences* are recognized because everyone progresses at his own rate. Don't be discouraged if another family member is seemingly progressing faster than you.

Talking to Your Child About Cuts and Germs

A word of caution for the parents and other caretakers of young children. When children move about, they occasionally fall. People used to simply kiss an "owie" to make it better and not think a thing about it. Today's world is much different with the advent of AIDS and the awareness of other transmittable diseases. Children need instruction of "what to do" when they are cut or when they play with someone who falls and bleeds. It can be a simple, relaxed, nonthreatening, and even fun way to learn about basic health. However, AIDS instruction for even the youngest child is of life-and-death importance.

Bubbly Bear

We recommend the following easy approach to instruction; it parallels health and safety instruction with a few important exceptions. Teach the lessons with the help of a stuffed bear. When the bear "talks" to your child, assume a different voice and make the bear move. Using a stuffed animal helps hold your child's interest and makes even the most serious discussions appealing.

1. "Here's a new friend to meet. His name is Bubbly Bear. He will tell us a story to help us stay healthy."
2. "Bubbly Bear says to wash your hands after you use the toilet and before you eat. Can you guess why? That's right—we can have germs on our hands, but if we wash with warm water and soap, the germs go away. Then the germs won't get inside us when we eat or if we put our fingers in our mouths." With a 4- or 5-year-old, you might even bring in sterile agar plates from a local hospital to show what germs look like: Grow a culture from dirt from under your child's fingernails, being sure to leave a control plate clean for comparison. Contaminate a third plate with freshly washed hands to show the difference in amount and kinds of germs. Tape the agar plates shut and label each one. Wait a few days, then observe the differences between freshly washed hands and dirty hands. A picture is worth 1,000 words.
3. "Bubbly Bear also knows another place where germs can hide. Sometimes germs can be in blood. We have blood inside us to help us grow. Its job is to carry food and air to all parts of the body. We need blood to live. [Point out a vessel on your child's hand.] Sometimes, though, if we fall or get cut, we make a small opening in the skin, and some blood comes out. Because some blood can also carry germs, it is best *not to touch* anyone else's blood. If a friend falls and bleeds, you can still help: Get a grown-up, and he or she can help fix the cut. Remember, Bubbly Bear says, 'Help your friend by getting a grown-up.' " You do not need to mention AIDS specifically or go into how it is otherwise contracted. Instead, simply caution your child *not to touch any bodily fluids.* You can limit your discussion to blood or, if the subject comes up, include other bodily fluids. The

ages and types of playmates that your child has will determine whether you might discuss other bodily fluids (urine,
vomit, tears, and saliva). The Health Information Network
says that the AIDS virus is found in small amounts in tears
and saliva but that *no* documented cases of transmission
from these fluids exist. You could simply caution your
child that adults can take care of any cleanup jobs that
need attention and that it's best not to touch anything wet
from a friend's body.

Caretakers involved in such cleanup should wear dispos-
able plastic gloves. Teachers in our school district wear
plastic gloves when treating cuts. They simply tell the children (not wanting to ostracize any individual children, the
teachers treat all of them with gloves), "Blood can carry
germs, so we wear these for protection against germs."
The children soon got used to the idea as part of school
health routines.

4. "Bubbly Bear also says, 'Be peaceful when playing.'" No
   pushing, no hitting, and no biting have always been good
   rules for groups of playing children. Good, old-fashioned
   discipline in structuring peaceful play periods is even more
   important today. We do not want to alarm you but to encourage you to reinforce basic health rules.

Ron Prichardt, an epidemiologist, says that the child who bites
is in more danger of contracting the AIDS virus than the one who
is bitten (unless the biter has bleeding gums). The Health Network states that *no* case has been known to have been transmit-
ted from one child to another in a school, day-care, or foster-care
setting. They further state that there is *no danger* of a child contracting AIDS from playmates: 80 percent of children with AIDS
were infected during pregnancy, 5 percent are hemophiliacs who
were treated with blood products before the need to check for and
destroy the virus was known, and 12 percent received transfu-
sions of infected blood in the course of other treatments. The
Public Health Service recommends that except in very unusual
circumstances, children with AIDS "should be allowed to attend
school and after-school day care and to be placed in a foster home
in an unrestricted setting." The AIDS virus is very fragile. Transmission requires direct exposure of the bloodstream to infected
blood, as for instance, if a child had a small cut on a finger and
touched the wound of an infected child. If your child just follows
Bubbly Bear's simple health rules (especially not to touch a play-
mate's blood but to be a friend by calling a grownup instead),
your child will be *safe* while having lots of fun.

Bubbly Bear also says to follow these guidelines:

- "Eat the food that is served to you, [the amount being determined by the child], not from other children's plates.
- "When drinking at a water fountain, let the water rise up to your lips—don't suck on the metal part of the fountain.
- "Spitting is *not* part of good health habits. Don't spit.
- "Keep your fingers out of your mouth. It is best not to suck your thumb or chew your nails because germs hide under your fingernails.
- "Take a bath when your parents tell you to. Germs are on our skin, but soap and warm water help them go away.
- "Brush your teeth: Then you'll be clean from tip to toe. Germs won't hide in that white stuff on your teeth [plaque] if you brush them off.

"Now that you are so squeaky clean, give me a big hug and go off to a good night's sleep because plenty of rest makes you strong to fight off whatever germs might be around. Sleep tight. Love from Bubbly Bear."

Being Fit for Fun

Sitting still does have its place in society. To make it easier for your child to adjust to this demand, though, alter what you require him to do just before and just after the time that you want him to sit still.

For a variety of reasons, today's children are much more sedentary than the children of 30 years ago. Parents, as children's first and foremost teachers, must instill in them a regular period of physical activity as a fun, habitual part of their daily lives. If parents do this, they will be helping their children to lead happier, healthier lives.

Infants can enjoy a variety of warm-up movements. Toddlers continue with the warm-ups but also add exploratory movement activities. Preschoolers build on these first two foundations of fitness but add a third dimension—sustained vigorous exercise. Follow Bubbly Bear's suggestions for staying well. Follow the suggested guidelines during the activity period. Choose from the variety of activities listed, and you will find that it is fun and easy to help yourself and your child develop and maintain fitness. So, get ready, set, grow! Be fit for fun!

PART II

Making Good Nutrition a Lifelong Habit

You probably remember hearing your parents saying "Clean Your Plate" more than once at the dinner table. Although you were pleasantly full and ready to quit eating, they insisted that you eat every last bite.

Many people retain the habit of cleaning their plates into adulthood. They feel guilty, consciously or unconsciously, when they leave small portions of food on their plate. Some may even carry it to extremes, not being able to tolerate food being left on others' plates, nibbling off any plate as they clear the table and do the dishes. Some experts say that this is a common reason that mothers slowly become overweight. Although this may sound unbelievable or humorous, it happens with frequency.

How much healthier it would be to establish correct eating habits right from the start. These habits will nurture a person for a lifetime of health and happiness rather than overweight and guilt. Not only how much is eaten but also how and what is eaten are important considerations.

In previous chapters the concept that intelligence can be enhanced by engaging in creative exploration and movement was introduced. Good nutrition also plays an important role in your child's intellectual and total development. In this section we will explore different aspects of providing proper nutrition for infant, toddler, and preschooler.

We begin in chapter 5 exploring children's natural inclinations toward food choices. Given a choice, would children choose a healthy diet? Are there things you can do as a parent to increase your child's chance of making proper selections? What kind of feeding schedule should she be on?

Chapter 6 examines influences that stand in the way of making good choices, such as commercials for junk food and social rewards of food. How do you prepare your child to deal with these and other inevitable factors?

Just as we presented alternatives to sitting still, chapter 7 presents alternative strategies to having your child 'clean her plate'. In chapter 8 we are excited to share with you nutritious recipes we have gathered from parents over the years. These recipes will help make your job of planning creative, well-balanced meals for your child easier. Nutritional content is included for each recipe so you can be assured that the recipes are dietetically balanced as well as kid-tested for good taste.

Chapter 5

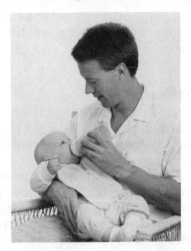

A Child's Natural Inclination to Choose a Healthy Diet

Eating patterns in the first 2 years of life are likely to persist for several years or a lifetime (Behrman & Vaughn, 1983). Fortunately, studies have also shown children (including infants) presented with nutritionally sound choices over a period of several days select adequate and well-balanced diets. Thus, strong likes and dislikes for particular foods should be respected whenever possible and practical and as long as the eating history is adequate over the longer period. Under normal circumstances, the child can be given the opportunity to determine the quantity of both a given food and the entire meal.

Spinach is an example of a food whose virtues have been over-emphasized. True, it is dark green and leafy, but several other green or yellow vegetables can provide vitamin A. Suggesting that your child sample a tiny, "Smurf-size" portion is preferential to force-feeding a large quantity. When she is older, you can

examine together the taste buds on her tongue with a magnify-
ing glass and explain which buds react to which type of foods
and why what tastes bad today may taste delicious tomorrow.
At this early stage of development, your child's eating habits may
also be influenced by older children, particularly in regard to food
likes and dislikes. When basics such as milk and eggs are
consistently rejected, though, the possibility of a food allergy
should be considered.

Prenatal Nutrition

The child's natural inclination to absorb as much as she requires
is established long before birth. The child absorbs from her
mother's body as many nutrients as she needs and as the mother
can provide. Hundreds of studies with pregnant women and
experimental animals show that the choices of food made by the
mother both *before* and during pregnancy determine the health
of the baby. The baby takes what it requires as long as the
nutrients are present in the mother.

A study by doctors from the School of Public Health at Harvard
University along with the prenatal clinic of Boston's Lying-In
Hospital will demonstrate this. Women's typical diets were classi-
fied as being "Poor," "Good" or "Poor-Supplemented-to-Good."
Money, food, and social services were provided in the group that
had had poor diets (referred to as the "Poor-Supplemented-to-
Good" category). The social worker called to ascertain that the
mother, not other family members, got the food supplements.

The infants were examined at birth by pediatricians who were
unaware of the quality of the foods that the mothers had ingested.
Prenatal diets and the condition of the infants were correlated.
Eighty-seven percent of the mothers with "Good" or "Poor-
Supplemented-to-Good" diets gave birth to infants in "good" or
"excellent" condition. In comparison, 95 percent of the infants
of "Poor Diet" mothers were found to be in "poor" or "extremely
poor" condition. The "extremely poor" group included stillborn
infants, those who died within a few hours or days of birth, feeble-
minded or retarded infants, and those with cleft palates, congenital heart defects, or congenital cataracts. The group classified as
being in "poor" condition included babies with tumors, eye
abnormalities, clubbed feet, and skin infections.

Clearly, the unborn baby takes food from her mother, and there
must be sound nutrition in the mother from which the baby can
draw. Therefore, the first rule of a baby's good nutrition is her

sound nutrition before being born. The mother's food habits before and during pregnancy are thus crucial.

In another study on the effects of a nutrition program during pregnancy, the group that had inadequate intake of nutrients and inadequate weight gain had a higher percentage of pregnancy-induced hypertension and premature labor complications. This same group had low-birthweight infants with a higher mortality rate and an increased incidence of mental retardation, visual and hearing defects, learning problems and disabilities, cerebral palsy, neurological defects, and poor growth and development. The group that had higher maternal weight gains and that ate to prescription gave birth to babies with fewer of these complications (Sweeney et al., 1985).

The time for good nutrition is all through pregnancy and, indeed, all through life. Mothers really are eating for two. A moderate but adequate amount of food is the key to good nutrition in pregnancy (later sections will discuss the dangers of overeating and how obesity develops).

It is apparent that sound nutrition affects the child physically, but it also affects her total development, including intellectual growth. Her brain reaches its peak of growth during the 3 months before birth and the first 6 months after birth. (Growth of the brain then continues slowly until age 4; after this period, the brain increases little or none in size.) Deficiencies in diet cause the most harm during these periods of greatest brain growth.

The mother who follows normal, nutritional eating patterns as recommended by her doctor (details can be found in such sources as the Essentials of Nutrition and Diet Therapy [Williams, 1985]) will quite naturally provide her infant with the nutrients needed. An optimal weight gain of approximately 11 kilograms (25 pounds or more, as needed) is recommended for pregnancy to accommodate fetal and placental growth, increased tissue weight in uterus and breasts, amniotic fluid, increased blood volume, and maternal stores of adipose tissue. Unfortunately, many pregnant women become overly concerned with how they look, whereas the ultimate goal of good prenatal care should be the health of the unborn infant and mother. This is NOT the time to be on a weight-loss program (except under a doctor's recommendation); it *is* the time for good, sound nutrition.

The nutritional quality is of even more significance than the actual weight gain. Increased amounts of protein, calcium, vitamin A, iron, folacin (a B vitamin), and vitamin C are needed. Careful attention to the mother's nutrition is called for during pregnancy and lactation.

The brain will not develop to its fullest potential without good pre- and postnatal nutrition. The earlier a deficiency occurs, the greater the amount of damage that is done. The brain can withstand severe dietary deprivations or even starvation once it is fully developed; although it may be severely affected at the time, the brain can return to normal when the diet of the fully developed person is improved. However, the developing brain does not have this ability to return to normal. Studies have shown that the poorer the nutrition, the smaller the brain as well as less DNA, RNA, and protein. The amount of DNA, a nucleic acid that carries hereditary patterns and helps synthesize the body's protein in every cell from conception onward, normally rapidly increases until the time of birth. DNA continues to increase slowly until 6 months of age, then very little from that time on (Davis, 1972).

A child born with normal intelligence can have brain damage caused by inadequate diet. This can happen anytime during the first 4 years, but the most vulnerable times are within the first 6 months. Simply following your doctor's recommendations for a nutritionally adequate diet will help your child reach her total genetic potential—physically, emotionally, and intellectually. The following pages give insight and ideas as you follow your doctor's suggestions.

Establishing Feeding Schedules

Prior to the 1940s, many babies were fed "by the clock" rather than when they were hungry. Researchers then discovered that babies would establish their own schedules if they were breastfed when they seemed hungry. They found that the babies woke infrequently during the first few days of life. In the remainder of the first week, just about the same time that the mothers began to produce milk, each baby woke surprisingly often—about 10 times a day. By 2 weeks, when the milk supply was well established, the number of feedings had settled to 6 or 7 a day, but they were at somewhat irregular intervals. Finally, by 10 weeks, each baby had established an approximate 4-hour schedule. The subjects had established the desired 4-hour schedule on their own as milk supply and tiny tummy size increased. What a much more comfortable way for the baby to adjust to the world than to be placed on an immediate, adult-set schedule.

Further study revealed that a flexible schedule of feedings did not lead to diarrhea or indigestion, nor to spoiling the child.

Instead, many feeding problems were eliminated before they ever had a chance to start.

Feeding on Demand

Demand, or letting infants regulate when they are ready to be fed, is a sensible approach to their changing needs. This self-regulation does not insinuate that parents' needs will not be considered. There may be times when you find it more convenient to wake your baby for a feeding after 3 hours of sleeping. There may be other times when you have to extend the time between feedings. Demand feeding provides you greater freedom to use your own judgment than did earlier "by-the-clock" approaches to infant care.

Babies seem to instinctively know when they have had enough. If breast-feeding, they pull away from the breast; if bottle-feeding (which has the added plus of involving Dad), they push the bottle away. Do not force your baby to eat more because she hasn't nursed "long enough" or because she hasn't taken the right number of ounces. This can only hurt her natural inclinations toward a healthy appetite. Depending on how long she has slept since her last feeding (and depending on other factors in her changing body and changing external environment), your baby will judge how much she needs at a particular feeding. Breast-fed babies usually nurse 10 to 15 minutes on each breast. Because the flow of milk varies, the time needed for your baby to get full will also vary.

In regulating the factor of time, remember to adjust supply to need. Overfeeding with breast or bottle can cause gas to the point of excess spitting or discomfort. Other possible factors, such as a natural tendency to spit up, gas, personality differences, and even your baby's being sensitive to anxiety on the part of the feeder tend to complicate the issue. Fortunately, these issues tend to resolve themselves with your intuitive use of good judgment and a little help from the baby's doctor.

Setting a Schedule

Subtly getting your baby to adjust to your family's time framework is often needed. Even the infant herself takes an active part in the give-and-take of close personal relationships. Dr. T. Berry Brazelton, associate professor of pediatrics at Harvard and chief of the Child Development Unit at Boston's Children's Hospital, endorses this approach (1983). A schedule that is too hectic, that quickly changes, or that doesn't settle into a routine calls for a consultation with your baby doctor for possible formula or diet changes (Spock, 1971). The diet of the mother can be another significant factor in how much the baby is interested in consuming. Let the baby judge how much will be consumed. Don't try to make her clean her plate even before she has a plate to clean.

Supplemental feedings with water (not sugar water) in hot weather can calm a thirsty, fussy baby. Fussing does not always indicate hunger, so search for other possible causes of her discomfort. Dr. Brazelton says that some babies should not be fed entirely on demand (1983). He feels that a restless, fretful baby may lead to a great many feedings and, therefore, little rest for the parents. Dr. Benjamin Spock (1971) feels that if a baby wakes early and finishes every bottle, the pediatrician should be consulted for increasing or changing the formula. With a breast-fed baby, the amount is easily determined by the child (Caplan, 1977).

If your baby wakes an hour or so after her last feeding, she probably isn't hungry but is more likely perturbed by indigestion or colic. Try burping her or offering some water or a pacifier, as well as holding and rocking her. If she is crying at what seem to be the wrong times, study the situation and consult your pediatrician or general practitioner.

Flexible feeding scheduling is desirable for most baby-parent relationships. It encourages parents to sensitize themselves to their babies' needs. It encourages a relaxed personality formation in the babies. It also lets them establish how much nourishment is needed right from the start.

Breast or Bottle?

Breast milk is the best food for normal infants during the first 5 to 6 months of life because it adapts in composition to meet the needs of the developing child. It has the specific characteristics that match the infant's nutritional requirements. A diet of breast milk alone for the first months is recommended for good nutrition; some experts even recommend it through the first year of life (Williams, 1985). Breast-feeding is successfully initiated by 99 percent of the women who try the process. The pediatrician should be consulted as to when there might possibly be a need to provide vitamin K, vitamin D, iron, or fluoride as supplements.

There is a variety of infant formulas approximating the composition of human milk that can also provide excellent nutrition, if you choose to bottle-feed. Your baby's doctor can recommend a commercial formula. Regular, unmodified cow's milk is *not* suitable for infants during the early months of life (Picciano, 1987). Furthermore, during the 1st year of life, infants should not consume milk of reduced fat content (skim or 2 percent) for two reasons: (a) it provides insufficient energy to support maintenance requirements; and (b) linoleic acid, an essential fatty acid contained in milkfat, is needed for growth and development of body tissues (Williams, 1985). Consult your baby's doctor as to the advisability of lowfat milk after the age of 1.

Current research indicates that there is no nutritional advantage to introducing solid foods earlier than 4 to 6 months. The exact time to introduce solid foods should be based on your infant's weight, the quality of milk being consumed (her doctor can judge this by comparing weight gains), the need for foods containing iron, her neuromuscular development, and by listening to her. Early introduction of solid food is rarely indicated; listen to your child and your child's doctor to know when it is right for your situation.

Introducing Solid Foods

Solid foods are usually added about the same time that the teeth begin to appear. Before your child's 1st birthday, she should be permitted a variety of ways of participating in the act of feeding. By 6 months or so, your infant can hold a bottle. Don't overuse this skill, losing out on building up the closeness of your relationship by your feeding her. Instead, let your infant try this new skill sometimes, but not as a general rule. Within another 2 to 4 months, your child can hold a cup. Zwieback, graham crackers, or other hand-held foods can be introduced by the age of 7 to 8 months. (A word of caution: Make sure these food items cannot be easily choked on—like carrot sticks or nuts can.) Your child may use a spoon as soon as she can hold it and direct it toward her mouth.

Try not to inhibit this learning process because of your objection to its messiness. Spreading a large plastic or other washable cloth under your baby's high chair can prevent a lot of stress on your part. Acquiring the ability to feed herself is an important step in your infant's development of self-reliance. By the end of her 2nd year, your infant should be largely responsible for her own feeding.

However, self-feeding should *not* include permitting your child to go to sleep while holding and intermittently sucking on a bottle, no matter whether it's filled with formula, milk, fruit juice, or even water. Pedodontists have called attention to the correlation of this habit and the bacterial erosion of the enamel in deciduous (baby) teeth. This "baby bottle syndrome" is caused by the increased formation of lactic and other acids that are harmful to dental enamel (Behrman & Vaughan, 1983).

Self-Feeding

Thus begins the marvelous, mature-but-messy stage of development marked by self-feeding. At this time, as when your baby first learned to suck, chew, and swallow, you parents should be patient, consistent, and relaxed. Overconcern by the parent is sensed by the child. Getting the baby to eat, in a variety of ways, just to get a certain amount ingested, is asking for problems and resistance. About 10 to 15 minutes of self feeding is actually sufficient. If your baby loses interest, it is time to stop. Similarly as when you nursed her, don't try to make her clean her plate. Remember, you are establishing habits that will last a lifetime.

By 6 months, your baby can eat just about anything the rest of the family does, provided that it has a texture that she can handle. Use a blender or a food processor (there is a small, hand-held type that grinds up food for babies) to make baby food quickly and easily. (Give a food processor to new parents as a baby gift.) If you process your own table food, your baby can enjoy a variety of healthful foods without any of the added sugar, salt, and preservatives often found in commercially prepared baby food.

You may want to purchase a few jars of commercially made baby food, though, because they are convenient for traveling. It is interesting to note that the commercial baby food companies are reflecting recent interest in health: Many offer lower amounts of salt or sugar. Check labels when you buy baby food.

Another baby-feeding tip is to save time by cooking and straining a large quantity of vegetables and fruits at one time. Freeze them in ice cube trays, then store the cubes in plastic bags in your freezer for later use. When needed, a single cube can be conveniently reheated for a feeding.

Naturally Good Choices

An experiment was conducted some years ago by Adele Davis, nutritionist and author (Davis, 1972). Her purpose was to determine what foods children would eat if left to their own desires.

Rather than selecting older children with previously established food likes and dislikes, she chose 18 orphans, all 6 months of age. Their previous diets had been nothing but milk. At every meal, their nurse would allow them to choose from six to eight serving dishes containing a variety of wholesome, unrefined foods, including fruits, vegetables, eggs, meats, cereals, whole grain breads, milk, water, and fruit juices. The nurses waited until the babies indicated what they wanted before assisting them to eat. Davis found that over a period of time each baby selected a well-balanced diet.

Other leading authorities also agree that if given a free choice, children will eat what they require and round out their dietary needs within a short time. Adults do likewise: They crave orange juice when they have colds. Thus, given appropriate choices (i.e., not having to choose between ice cream and candy bars but rather between meat and vegetables), your infant will choose a balanced diet. Therefore, you shouldn't worry if she isn't eating a particular vegetable for a while. The likes and dislikes for certain foods vary with age. Just provide her with well-balanced choices.

Toddlers and preschoolers, if presented with appealing nutritional choices, also choose balanced diets over a period of time. You are well aware that if the choices include sweets, the child will choose the sweetened food. Thus, simply don't include sweets among the choices. Instead, we found that if we offered two or three vegetables and two or three fruits at an evening meal, each of our children would be able to find at least one fruit and one vegetable that he or she really liked. We also encouraged them to try new things but didn't force them to eat a particular amount.

We noticed an interest in our children at a young age in lots of foods, then less tolerance for variety as they approached age 5. We would all look at our tongues when they were preschoolers and try experiments such as finding which taste buds seemed to enjoy sour or salty foods (at the sides of the tongue) and which buds relished sweet tastes (at the tip of the tongue). We would look at buds and notice whether new buds were forming. We discussed the idea that because taste buds are developing at all stages, if the children didn't care for a particular food at age 2, they should be willing to try it again at 3.

Visiting Your Doctor

With proper nutrition in utero as well as during early childhood, intellectual as well as general physical growth can be maximized.

Good nutrition is natural and easy to provide. Malnutrition may result from inadequate or improper food intake or from inadequate absorption of food. Poor dietary habits, food faddism, deficient supply of food, or emotional factors may limit the intake of food.

Precise evaluation of nutritional status is difficult. Severe disturbances are readily apparent, but even after careful observation by the nonprofessional, mild disturbances may be overlooked. This is why it is important to follow through with frequent visits to your child's doctor during the first years of life. The doctor is the best one to diagnose whether nutritional needs are being met. He or she does this by careful observations of an accurate dietary history, comparison to average age-group weight, height and head-circumference measurements, comparison to past rates of growth, comparative measurements of midarm circumference and skinfold thickness, and results from chemical tests. The doctor is trained to determine whether your child is developing normally.

Height, Weight, and Other Measures of Health

During the periodic exams, ask to see your child's progress on a height-weight graph. Keeping the ratio within normal limits is desirable. This is an important factor that will increase her chance for a long life, according to Atlanta's Center for Disease Control. Indeed, they say that 52 percent of all early deaths are related to various lifestyle factors (Pooling Project, 1978).

These percentages are on the rise. C. Everett Koop, U.S. Surgeon General, says that Americans are eating their way to early grave. What we eat (especially too much fat and salt) may affect our risk for the following disorders: coronary heart disease, stroke, atherosclerosis, diabetes, and some types of cancer. These disorders now account for two-thirds of all deaths in the USA ("Americans Eating Their Way," 1988). Thus, such lifestyle factors as keeping weight within the normal range and using those seatbelts will give your child better chances for a longer life.

You and your doctor should determine together whether your child's height-weight ratio is within the normal range. Neither an obese nor an ultrathin look is recommended. It is important to have accurate records and a reference point relative to height and weight to be able to check your child's progress through the years.

Your doctor also checks what is going on internally with blood and urine tests. Recent studies are revealing that cholesterol problems begin in childhood. If your family has a history of heart problems, your doctor might also include a blood lipid report. This will let you know how able your child's blood is to fight off heart disease factors. Even a very thin child (or adult) can have elevated cholesterol levels, which can lead to premature death. Thus, the doctor's complete examination is important—you can't always judge a book by its cover. Periodic checkups help ensure normal development.

Normal Development

The first 2 years of life are characterized by amazing growth. Let your doctor be the one to determine whether your child is developing normally. You can relax and marvel as you observe these normal changes. During the first few days of life, infants lose weight. By the 7th to 10th day, though, the birth weight is usually regained. Thereafter, growth proceeds at a rapid yet decelerating rate. Infants' birth weight is usually doubled by 4 months and tripled by 1 year. The 2nd year's weight gain approximates the birth weight. Infants increase their length by 50 percent in the 1st year of life and double it by 4 years of age.

Changes occur not only in height and weight but also in the actual composition of the tissue. Nitrogen content of the body increases from 2 percent of body weight at birth to 3 percent by 4 years of age. Body fat increases rapidly during the first 9 months, but the increments of fat-gain steadily decline during the remainder of childhood. Total body water decreases from 70 percent at birth to 60 percent at 1 year. With such tremendous changes occuring, sound nutrition is essential. Also of prime importance are the doctor's observations of the child to ensure that these tremendous changes are occuring normally.

The first years are characterized by rapid physical, mental, social, and emotional growth and development. These are the years in which many changes that affect feeding and nutrient intake occur. The adequacy of the infant's or young child's intake of nutrients affects her interaction with the environment. When the child is healthy and well nourished, she has the energy to respond to and learn from the environmental stimuli and respond to her parents in a manner that encourages bonding and love.

As a parent and a caretaker, make the effort to keep your child's nutrition at least adequate. Your child will more likely fulfill her genetic potential. You child's nutrition and how to ensure it in ways that are palatable and fun for her will be the focus of the following chapters of this book.

Chapter 6

Influences Inhibiting a Child's Natural Inclination to Make Healthy Food Choices

"Fat babies are healthy babies" is a well-known adage. Chubby babies may look cute, but they can turn into obese, unhappy, and unhealthy adults. Recent studies reveal that children's physiological makeup can be altered if they are fed excessive amounts of foods, especially fat-inducing foods. This chapter will consider such studies as well as some methods that have been used in the past to induce overeating.

Fat Cells and Fat Children

Dr. Jerome Knittle of the Mount Sinai School of Medicine and Dr. Fredda Ginsburg-Fellner studied 200 obese children between the ages of 2 and 18 (Davis, 1972). The doctors examined small samples of fat that were drawn from the children with a special syringe. Microscopic examination revealed that the number of fat cells in obese children was greatly higher than the number of fat cells of children of normal weight. Some 5- and 6-year-olds had a higher number of fat cells than average-weight adults. There was reason to believe that if the children's diets were not restricted, their fat cells would continue to increase in size and number until some time after puberty.

Dr. Ginsburg-Fellner did an additional study to determine the effect of severe reducing diets on already obese children aged 2 to 10. These children all had been obese before age 1, and their weights were almost double the normal for their age and height. Following a severe reducing diet, each was put on a 1,200-calorie diet for up to 4 years. Some children (for example, a 2-1/2-year-old boy) were reduced to normal weight and maintained it for over 1 year. Others (for example, a 7-year-old girl who had 43 billion fat cells—1-1/2 times as many as the average adult) rapidly regained the weight lost by the diet, then weighed more than ever. These latter children have retained an excessive number of fat cells. They will most likely have to be on severe diets to lose weight and stay on moderate diets to stabilize for the rest of their lives.

There is more hope, however, for children who reduce before they have produced an excessively large number of fat cells. Dr. Ginsburg-Fellner believes that they have a fairly good chance of maintaining an ideal weight. However, the best hope of all comes from preventing that overabundance of fat cells from ever occurring! The child's first eating patterns are crucial.

Your Child's First Eating Patterns

To prevent the early onset of obesity, parents need to learn and establish sound feeding and related child care practices while their children are still infants and toddlers. Researchers have discovered that obese children follow a pattern of development that is different from nonobese children. By 2 years of age, obese children develop adipose (fat) cells that are of comparable size to those of nonobese adults. After this age, these children's fat stores continue to increase, largely because of increases in the number of adipose cells. In contrast, nonobese children gain little adipose tissue between 2 years and puberty (Pisacano, 1978).

Early Postnatal Feeding

Because nutrition can permanently affect the structure and function of many body organs, adequate caloric intake is still critical during the 1st year of life, when children grow, learn, and change at a quicker rate than at any other time. The goal for therapy for overweight infants, therefore, is weight control, not weight reduction. Ideally, the obese baby's weight will remain stable and he will "grow into" the correct weight for his size.

Early postnatal feeding practices influence children's entire lives (Committee on Nutrition, 1981). Expectant and new parents need to be informed on feeding practices; then many problems can be prevented. Too often, new parents believe that an infant's sucking reflex and crying always indicate hunger, regardless of when he was last fed. Feeding as an automatic response to the infant's distress signal is a habit to be avoided.

Offering Alternatives to Feeding

During infancy, offering a pacifier between feedings to satisfy a baby's sucking needs, a bathtub experience, a back rub, or a rocking session snuggled in your favorite chair can substitute for food when the baby appears distressed.

New parents need to also become familiar with the caloric values of infant foods. If your baby has been diagnosed as overly fat by the doctor, compare labels on baby food jars, or even better, prepare your own baby food. Remember that solids should not be introduced before 5 or 6 months; your infant's nutritional needs can be entirely met by breast milk or formula. Increased consumption of food makes no substantial contribution to your infant's diet and only creates poor eating habits (Pipes, 1984). You parents can also increase your interactions with your child and realize that he is awake more and animated at times other than when being fed or when hungry.

Your Attitudes and Your Child's Responses to Food

The power of your interactions lasts a lifetime. It is how your infant feels when you tell him the thousands of little things that he is doing right that can lead him to become a positive person. A fast-growing body of research (104 studies so far) is proving that an optimistic attitude can help one be healthier, happier, and more successful.

A pessimistic attitude, in contrast, leads to hopelessness, failure, sickness, and even depression (Safran, 1987). Frequently people with these problems resort to food as a way to relieve their anxiety. How much more well they can be if they have a positive attitude. It is a pattern of thinking that develops at very early ages. It grows out of thousands of encouragements or positive statements, rather than an equal number of cautions or negative statements. Some don'ts and warnings are necessary, but too many of them can make a child feel incompetent, pessimistic, and fearful. Positive thinking leads to positive action and reaction from others. The self-fulfilling prophecy exists.

The secret of success is to catch your infant doing something good, then let him know about it. If he is having a problem, seek alternate solutions together. Of course, there are times when a firm response is in order: If your child is running toward a busy street, you take action—you don't discuss solutions.

However, the rule generally applies. Let your child be aware of how wonderful he is. If you do, you won't find him wanting to escape life by eating as much junk food, avoiding exercise, losing himself in too much TV, having too much to drink, or otherwise ignoring a wellness approach to life as he grows up. Turn your child's small accomplishments into major successes, and he gains a sense of control and optimism. This can help avoid childhood or adult obesity and at the same time make him happier with life.

A Word About Television

Childhood obesity has increased dramatically during the past 15 to 20 years. Among 6- to 11-year-olds, it is 54 percent more prevalent. Television watching is a major contributor to this new trend. TV watchers are less active and are exposed to more food advertisements than those who watch limited TV. Watching TV even affects the metabolic rate. A study shows that watching TV produces a lowered rate at which the body functions; the food is burned off more slowly, and an almost hypnotic effect occurs (Blessing, 1986).

Although children of obese parents may be genetically predisposed toward overweight, they are not doomed to obesity. If the parents follow the suggestions included here and consult their baby's doctor, children can resist the influences that would lead them toward this health problem and move instead toward a well way of life.

The "Clean Your Plate" Attitude

The "clean your plate" attitude establishes bad habits that last a lifetime. A parent who tries to make a child take one more mouthful just because it is left in the baby food jar is establishing in the child a response of eating all that is there, no matter what the amount. Some adults find that no matter how much is in the serving dish, they will eat and eat until it is completely gone.

Once the habit is established, there are some ways to help someone thus afflicted. Prepare smaller amounts of food. Otherwise, have him dish up his portion, but then remove the serving dishes from the table. Another idea is to do the dishes together, so that the one with the bad habit is not doing them alone, where he may be tempted clean off the plates to his heart's delight (does it really delight his heart? No!).

Misguided Encouragements and Games

There are several "cute" tricks that parents have to make a baby take that last bite, even if satiated. There is the airplane that vvrrrrooooms its way into the hangar (mouth) and the train that chug-a-chug-a-chugs along the track. The varieties of tricks are endless. Can it be any wonder that the child carries this over into adulthood and is compulsively overweight? The child who grows up into the obese adult is no longer cute, nor are the health problems that accompany obesity.

Even the schools tried to proselytize the philosophy that plates must be cleaned. Recall the days that kindergartens promoted a "Clean Plate Club," where parents reported whether their children practiced this policy. Here, cleaning the plate was actually taught as part of the "health" curriculum. Was this really helping the child's health?

The Wrong Rewards for the Wrong Attitudes

If parents use the ploy "You can't have dessert until you eat your vegetables," aren't they really making the dessert seem more desirable by using it as a reward? In our home, we like to encourage fruits for dessert, and we only occasionally have a sweeter treat—for example, a low-calorie cake for birthdays. There are also several ways you can cut down on sweets and still make inviting desserts, as you will see in the last chapter of this book. If you are always offering the sweeter kind of dessert, ask yourself whether it isn't really you who prefers it, not your child.

Cookie Monsters

The Cookie Monster on TV's *Sesame Street* is a beloved favorite of children, yet he, as well as numerous other audiovisual stimuli, promotes a monstrous addiction to sweetened food. It is true that the Cookie Monster occasionally appears on a commercial that promotes the four basic food groups. However, here a whole truckload of cookies falls on him for devouring after he eats the good food. This attempt to popularize the four basic foods is aired on TV with considerably less frequency than the other Cookie Monster scenes where he devours only sweets.

Sugar Advertising and National Consumption

Our Cookie Monster friend is not the only promoter of sweets whose target is the young listener. Watch TV on Saturday morning with your child and count up the numerous inducements for sweetened cereals, sugar-loaded candies, and pastries. Then the next time you walk down certain aisles at the grocery store, feel the pressure that these young listeners exert on you to buy certain products. The commercials do their jobs very well. Sometimes a symphonic tune that accompanies a waterfall of syrup pouring over luscious fruits, pancakes, and waffles can induce salivation without even a spoken word.

Cigarette ads were banned from TV years ago because of their deleterious influence. Health warnings are placed upon cigarette packages. Further bans are being proposed today. Perhaps similar warnings and restrictions should be placed on sugar and fat advertising "monsters" that attack children.

A number of studies have been done that verify the justification for such warnings. Sugars today make up 20 percent to 25 percent of the calories and 50 percent of the carbohydrates of the typical American diet. These sugars are hidden in numerous, everyday products, including commercial baby foods (are they trying to make it more delectable for the infant or for the mother who nibbles a bit from the baby's jar?), canned fruits, yogurt, and even frozen vegetables, as well as the more obviously sweetened foods like sodas and baked desserts.

How Does Sugar Affect Your Child's Health?

Dr. Jean Mayer, who was professor of nutrition at Harvard from 1950 to 1976 and is now president of Tufts University, has expressed a strong position on the use of sugar. In reviewing the following findings, Dr. Mayer has concluded that consuming large amounts of sugar habitually is a menace to health (1976).

Sugar and Cavities

Ninety-eight percent of American children have some dental caries. About half of all Americans at age 55 have no teeth. A recent government study indicates that sugar consumption is positively related to tooth decay.

Sugar and Overweight

Recent statistics show that 10 percent to 20 percent of all U.S. children and 35 percent to 50 percent of all middle-aged Americans are overweight. Sixteen percent or less of body weight should be fat in the average man; 23 percent is the average for women. These percentages are determined by underwater weighing, by skinfold measurements on various parts of the body, or by electronic impedance analysis machines. Percentages that are much higher than these define the individual as "overfat." Foods that provide empty calories (i.e., no nutrients) are a major factor in causing overfat.

Sugar and Disease

Overweight in general and sugar specifically are found to be related to hypertension and to adult-onset diabetes. The possible relationship between sugar and hyperactivity in children is still under study; this issue should be monitored for future results.

We do not advocate the complete elimination of sugar but rather a judicious watchfulness on sugar intake in its varied forms. Important weight gains can be made without the over-abundant use of sugar. True—hospitals give sugar in the water to newborns to help avoid early low blood sugar (hypoglycemia). Yet, what is appropriate for newborn children is too often copied by mothers after the child comes home from the hospital. Additional sugar in the water is not needed after those first few days. Prepared formulas and even breast milk have some sugar in them. Added sugar in water or, later, in food entices even the youngest infant to develop a taste for sweets. Careful awareness of sugar intake from the first few days of life onward will aid your child in his healthy development.

School and Societal Influences

A visit to your child's preschool, nursery school, or day care will quickly tell you what type of snacks and meals are being served. Are they nutritious or just filling or sugar-laden? You might suggest changes to the director or the parent could volunteer to bring in healthful snacks for a "tasting party." Encourage other parents to follow suit. We have included a nutrition unit every year during Heart Month, February. Children are never too young to start learning the importance of eating from the four basic food groups. Young children enjoy graphing to see which food group is the most popular. We have found the bread group usually wins. This leads right into discussions of what would happen if people ate from only one food group.

Societal functions and family gatherings also influence children's early habits which will last a lifetime. We were pleased to see our church serve popcorn and juice for the bulk of the snack at a recent Christmas party (Santa did pass out candy canes). The main thing to encourage with groups is not to abstain from sweets completely but to provide choices that include nutritional items along with a limited number of sweet items. Do not try to delete sweets completely; rather, delete sweets from your child's diet in general. Our goal has been not to have our children feel that they were "health nuts" but that in group or family situations they would eat nutritious foods as a general rule.

As our children continued into elementary school, we enjoyed watching health habits that were begun early occasionally even carry over to their friends. We recall when they invented a contest with their friends to eliminate sugars of any "added" variety for 1 week. We joined in by offering a visit to a nearby state park to all the "winners." Parents called and told how their children were reading labels and breezing through or struggling through the week. Families became more nutrition-conscious. "Pizza at the Park" on the following Saturday was enjoyed by several families. What was the most fun of all was that the children had started the idea themselves.

Other family and societal functions should always provide some nutritional choices. An angel food birthday cake served only with strawberries can hold candles just as easily as a store-bought iced one. We can recall taking our children to a bakery to show them the lard that goes into the frosting, which made the frosting much less desirable to them. Food is usually a feature in any social gathering. A truly caring host or hostess will always provide nutritional choices—whether for children or adults.

Junk Food Junkies

Parents' attitudes toward food shape infants' tastes in foods. Early feeding habits are established by 2 years of age. If the parents have always provided balanced food choices that are attractive and palatable for the entire family, this crucial dietary habit will carry over into adolescence and adulthood. This is true not only for what is served at mealtimes but also for between-meal snacks. Even the child who is eating well at mealtime may need a mid-morning or mid-afternoon snack.

Unfortunately, this is when many parents give in to junk foods. Whether in the supermarket checkout lane, at the zoo, or at a shopping center, almost everywhere there are vending machines to entice the young child. Besides the colorful sights and intriguing noises the machines make, some junk foods even attract the sense of smell, as at donut stands. Junk foods are appealingly available in almost every location. Some are even located in schools, where parents have little control over what their children buy. You can even buy gumball machines and snow cone makers to set up in your own home, as if you didn't deal with enough of them in the outside world.

The emphasis is that nutritious choices should be available when your child is really hungry for a snack. If you acknowledge that this hungry time occurs and make sure more healthful choices are available, then your child won't have to give in to sneaking something that is not nutritious. (See traveling and snack food sections in chapter 8 for suggestions).

The same principle is true for whoever does the shopping for the family. If you have had a low-calorie snack before you go into the grocery store, you are less hungry and less likely to give in to the huge assortment of nonnutritious choices. To combat this deluge of junk food when shopping with your child, arm yourself ahead of time. Bring along your own healthful snacks, packaging them colorfully. If you are stuck in a long checkout line and your child is getting fretful, you then have something healthful to offer him.

Food Equals Love

Dr. Brazelton criticizes parents who give teething biscuits or cookies to fretful youngsters to quiet them down. During the toddler age, the spirit of adventure is frequently interrupted by attacks of anxiety. Hugs and kind words can go a lot further than food products in easing through these situations. Frequently, it seems that these bouts with anxiety come at awkward times. For example, one is more likely to give in while fixing supper. Family teamwork during such stressful times can help keep you from establishing a food-equals-love habit in your child. If he had a healthful snack an hour before, you would know that it is attention, not food, that is needed.

Grandparents and Other Relatives

Grandparents and other relatives are important in helping your child mature. At times, though, they may underplay their value or limited amount of time or attention and feel they should "make it up" with sweet treats so the child will remember them with love. How much more beneficial and lasting it would be for them to have an active experience together. Treating them to a simple sponge (or rubber) ball and making a game to go with it is a splendid gift that the child will remember forever. Playing with a colorful toy (bought or homemade), doing a puzzle, drawing, or picking out a good TV show and watching it together are alternatives for those who feel they lack the strength to become involved in more active play. Taking the child for a walk around the block or spreading a blanket in the grass and discovering the universe hiding in the grass can add memories of love. Those who have a green thumb can show off their gardens or reveal the wonders to be found in the woods or fields. When a child visits or you visit the child, bring some seeds and plant them together. Do an art project with the child.

Be creative. Whatever you would enjoy doing with your own child, try some of the same with your grandchild or niece or nephew. Time and attention are absolutely the most cherished and valuable gifts, whether you be parent, grandparent, relative, loving friend, or preschool educator. Time, not food, equals love.

You can't choose your relations, but you can choose the principal daytime caretaker of your child if you work outside the home. When making your selection, be sure to inquire as to the types of food that will be served, the schedule of feeding, the patterns of food use, and so on. Then make your decision as to who the caretaker will be —perhaps a relative, a day-care center, a nursery school, a preschool, or a babysitter. After you have made your choice, communicate clearly your desires in regard to your child. They are with him a large portion of the waking day. Make sure that their practices reflect what you believe in.

Divorce—Stress, Love, and Food

Divorce involves a lot of problems for parents and children. Food and eating can become one of the problems. Parents should recall their children's best interests and not use food as a weapon to keep the children on one's "side." Parents should keep communication going so that lack of adequate nutrition or the use of binge-type feeding does not begin to occur. The duty to be a good parent continues even if the marriage doesn't. The primary caretaker needs to communicate to the other the detailed eating routines and even menus that each child is used to. Thus, one part of his environment will remain stable even when he visits separate homes.

Failure-to-Thrive Babies

Nutritional requirements vary for each individual in regard to genetic and metabolic differences. Yet the goal is the same: satisfactory growth and avoidance of deficiency states as well as maintenance of a normal amount of weight. Good nutrition contributes to the prevention of acute and chronic illness and to the development of mental and physical potential. It also provides reserves for relieving stress. Although intake for good nutrition involves considerable variability, mild excesses of nutrients or calories may be as undesirable as mild deficiencies. Ideal weight is desired not only for aesthetic reasons but also to prevent such complications as shortness of breath, diabetes and early death (Behrman & Vaughn, 1983).

A word of caution is in order, lest some parents or caretakers become overly zealous in trying to limit calories and fat in young children. We have frequently said that moderation is the key. Obesity is a problem, but parents should not let the pendulum swing too much in the other direction, because that can also cause health problems. Drs. Michael Pugliese and Fima Lifshitz (1987) studied "failure-to-thrive" babies and found that these slowly growing children were consuming far too few calories. The poorly developing babies were from well-educated, suburban parents who were extremely interested in their restriction of fat and calories. Fortunately, once the children were put on higher calorie diets, they grew and made weight gains that were appropriate for their sex and age. For a truly well child, parents should not become obsessed with slimness but instead remember the prudence of moderation. Realizing our goal for the total wellness of the child, we will consider some alternative ideas to the influences that go against the child's total development.

Chapter 7

Helping Children Eat Right

The infant's taste for foods and her food habits are shaped by her parents' attitudes. Family diets and menus that encourage high-protein foods (such as lean meats, poultry, fish, cottage cheese and other cheeses, and soybeans), fruits, vegetables, milk, and high-fiber, whole grain breads and also discourage the three Ss (sugar, salt, and saturated fats) are essential to a child's health. The secret of success is to prepare balanced foods that are attractive, delicious, and even exciting to eat. Feeding habits are established by 2 years of age; this means parents have only a very short time to foster sound eating patterns that will carry over into adolescence and adulthood.

Nutritional Needs of Children

The nutritional requirements for normal growth change considerably from infancy through childhood and adolescence. During infancy, the body grows faster than at any other time of life and the calorie and protein requirements per unit of body weight are high. The nutritional requirements for proper growth and development continue to change throughout childhood. The Food and Nutrition Board of the National Academy of Sciences–National Research Council has set nutritional standards for infants and children. Table 7.1 should serve as a guideline to help you maintain good nutrition for your child.

The most basic nutrient need for every person is water. Approximately 70 percent of body weight is water. Water is the most abundant chemical in the body. Water is so vital to all body processes that thirst impels people to drink long before their "water level" becomes low.

Many times, however, people choose to quench their thirst with

Table 7.1
Daily Nutritional Guidelines for Children

Group	Age[a]	Calories[b]	Protein (grams)	Sodium (milligrams)
Infants	0- 6	550- 900	13	115- 350
	6-12	700-1,200	18	250- 750
Children	1- 3	1,300 (900-1,800)	23	325- 975
	4- 6	1,700 (1,300-2,300)	30	450-1,350
	7-10	2,400 (1,650-3,300)	34	600-1,800
Adolescents Males	11-14	2,700 (2,000-3,700)	45	900-2,700
	15-18	2,800 (2,100-3,900)	56	900-2,700
Females	11-14	2,200 (1,500-3,000)	46	900-2,700
	15-18	2,100 (1,200-3,000)	46	900-2,700

[a]Given in months for infants, years for the rest. [b]Figures in parentheses represent the general range.

something other than water. Your child should be encouraged to drink water instead of sweetened drinks. Milk and fruit juices are important, but offering your child water at other times is important; water drinking is a good habit to foster. Special attention should be given to infants and young children because their need for water is greater than at any other time of life. This is because of their rapid rate of growth and increased metabolic rate.

Infants need approximately 825 to 1,350 milliliters (3 to 5-1/2 cups) of water daily. Young children need 1,000 to 1,500 milliliters (1 to 1-1/2 quarts) daily. Adolescents need at least 2 liters (2 quarts) daily. Learning to drink water to quench thirst is a positive habit that will persist into adulthood.

Lead your child to nature's "fountain of youth"—water. One way to make water more appealing to your child is to serve it at the temperature that she prefers. Most infants prefer warmer water, whereas many toddlers and children choose cool or icy cold water.

Another way to foster the enjoyment of water is to allow the child to serve it herself at as young an age as possible. We filled a deep drawer that was at child level (i.e., near the floor) with unbreakable plastic cups. It became great fun for our children to help themselves to a cup and a cold drink of water from our water-in-the-door refrigerator. They loved the independence and got into a habit of drinking water at an early age. As you can guess, there were several spills as they mastered the technique, but it was worth it for the habit it fostered. If you have a regular refrigerator, you could still allow independence by placing a small pitcher of water on your refrigerator's lowest shelf. (One disadvantage: They have to be big enough to open the door.)

Creating a Relaxed Mealtime Atmosphere

Although nutrition is extremely important, eating is still also a social event, a time when children learn as family members. There is evidence that demonstrates that young children (or animals) raised in isolated environments develop poorly, even if well fed. It is important to keep the mealtime atmosphere pleasant and relaxed. The infant who is forced to drink more or the toddler who has to eat the entire amount predetermined by an adult finds the feeding situation one of stress. Force feeding can turn mealtime into a battleground of nerves rather than an enjoyable part of daily life.

Encourage Early Independence

It is generally a good idea to let your youngster take over her own feeding as early as she seems interested. Finger foods start the path toward self-feeding. If both you and your child simultaneously enjoy the use of a spoon, this encourages independence. When your child begins to grab at your feeding spoon, hand her one to experiment with while you continue to feed her with yours. Remain watchful for cues that she is full.

Later, when your child eats quite independently, she can help decide how much she will eat. When she can verbalize the idea, have her help decide how big a portion she would like: teeny-weeny, a great big bite, or somewhere in between. Letting your child help decide and encouraging smaller portions can help cut way down on wasted food. Parents understandably have negative feelings about food being left on plates, becoming wasted food, because of soaring grocery bills. These feelings are realistic, but the solution to the problem is simple. If you dish up smaller portions than you think your child will consume, then allow her to ask for more (she may just indicate nonverbally if too young to ask), you won't waste much food at all. Furthermore, you will have a healthier child. Your child then eats because she is hungry, not because she is compelled to eat. Use yet smaller portions when dishing up seconds; then any leftovers will be minimal. In any case, don't let your concern for your meal's waste go to your family's waist!

Later, when your child is able, allow her to dish up her own small portions. Encourage her to judge how much she will like. Don't allow negativism to crush her ability to judge when her first estimations aren't quite right. Even a grown-up sometimes admits, "My eyes were bigger than my stomach."

Some children may try to abuse the freedom of choice that they are allowed. They may ask for only very small portions or say they have had enough, only to return to the kitchen shortly after supper asking for sweets. If they try this trick with treats, it would be wise to either retain the dinner food for when they return (pop it in the microwave to quickly reheat) or provide only snacks that are as delicious and nutritious as your meal was. We prefer the first method, for our children soon learned that they might as well have eaten dinner with the others—and we like to encourage the family to eat together as a unit. The second method, in contrast, tends to discourage a family mealtime because of the ready availability of food at any time.

Plan Relaxed Mealtimes

Another idea to help create relaxed self-feeding is to prolong the meal. Encourage a nonrushed atmosphere so that your child's partially full stomach has a chance to send a message to her brain that it is getting full. It usually takes several minutes for her to get this message. If your family gulps down the meal in a few minutes, seconds, thirds, and overeating usually result. Adults and children alike haven't had time to realize that they are satiated.

Good old-fashioned family conversation about the day's events can help slow the meal down. As children get older, it seems that everyone wants to talk at once. We have found it fun to use a wooden spoon as a makeshift "microphone." This helps ensure the speaker's uninterrupted time to tell of her day's happenings. The spoon's presence also placates the others who are waiting, because they realize that the spoon will be passed to them in a minute or two. Turning the TV off before the meal starts aids both in enhancing awareness of the enjoyable act of eating (which in turn provides more satisfaction with what is eaten), as well as in creating undivided attention to family conversation. The family can leave the table with emotional, as well as physical, satisfaction.

Encouraging Help in the Kitchen

As your child grows in independence and responsibility, encourage her to help in preparing the meal, setting the table, and cleaning up. We are always developing the whole child. Her good nutrition is interlocked with her physical, intellectual, and social growth. Besides establishing good eating habits by active involvement in meal preparation, she also grows intellectually. In helping you cook, she can see the need for learning how to read and for studying measurements and math. In setting the table, she gains practice in sorting and counting and in distinguishing such things as left and right. In clearing the table, she learns about neatness and orderliness. In helping to put away the dishes, she gains experience in classifying.

Of course, you would not have her help with everything; when she is young, have her help with what interests her most. This makes helping the family a fun part of life that grows into real responsibility as years go by. Thus, if you would visit our home, it would not be uncommon to see a one or two-year-old cracking eggs (have her do it in a separate bowl; then you can fish out the shell pieces that slipped in), helping stir, or putting away cans from the grocery sacks. Now, we must admit, that it is lots easier for you to do these things yourself (and much less messy, too). However, by the time your child is 4 or 5 years old, she is truly a big help. In all of these things, your child should be actively involved.

This kind of involvement with food can even aid the balky eater. All it takes is time and patience on your part. Parents need not worry about "problem eaters" if they realize that rates of development (and therefore need for food) occur normally as the child matures.

During the 1st year, infants grow rapidly. In the years between infancy and adolescence, their rate of growth slows and is even erratic. During some periods there are plateaus of growth, whereas other periods involve spurts of growth. The overall rate affects appetite in a corresponding manner. At times children have little or no appetite, whereas at other times they will eat voraciously. Parents can relax and not make mealtimes a battleground if they realize that these patterns are normal (Williams, 1985).

Junking Junk Foods

Don't buy junk foods. If you already have them in your home, throw them out. They are not even fit to give to your dog. If these kinds of foods are not in your home, the young (or older) nibbler won't be tempted to eat them. Avoid places outside your home that entice you to buy. Detour around the "Snack Shack." Hurry by the candy counter. Do not go to the store when you are hungry; that is the time when you are most likely to give in to the audiovisual inducements to buy. Either skip, or concentrate on the opposite side of, the sweets aisles at the grocery store. If you don't see something, chances are you won't want it.

Avoid Refined Foods

Avoid as many refined foods as possible. These include all white-flour products and presweetened cereals. Some foods, such as ice creams and certain bakery products, obviously contain large amounts of sugar. Other foods are deceptive; they have lots of sugar but it isn't as obvious. These include synthetic fruit drinks containing sugar, dyes, and chemical flavorings but little or no real fruit juice.

All you really have to do to find the culprits is to read the fine print on the labels. See which items list sugar as a prime ingredient. (It is gratifying when older children scrutinize a label in the store for themselves, notice that sugar is the first and most prevalent ingredient, then reject the product). Read the labels and you will see the countless items that contain added sugar. Words ending in -ose indicate that the item contains a type of sugar. Some examples are dextrose, sucrose, maltose, glucose, lactose, and fructose.

Talk to Your Child About Labels

Help your child to understand what the higher amounts of sugar can do to her. Help her to be a sugar detective and become able to identify it under its variety of labels (sugar, sucrose, dextrose, honey, corn syrup, etc.). It can also help her math ability as she compares which of two ingredients is "more" or "less." Then when you limit the amount of what we call the "candy cereals," your child will understand why. Compare the nutrition information for Nabisco's Shredded Wheat and "Sugar Yukkies" on the labels on page 110. Especially note the ingredients and the carbohydrate information[1]. You can see that the "Sugar Yukkies" are definitely not as healthy for your child—or yourself—as the other cereal is.

We, as parents, realize how the children are deluged with sugar cereal commercials. A countermeasure we found to work was that we generally did not buy any high-sugar-content cereals. However, so that such cereals would not become overly alluring, we allowed each child to choose a cereal on her birthday. What they all soon discovered was that these cereals didn't taste as great as the commercials said. Thus, if they never had it, it would be all the more appealing; yet, by being limited to a few boxes a year, they soon discovered that there was little more than a fancy box and a high-interest commercial. Often, I could make hot oatmeal or Cream of Wheat just as alluring if I would tell the story of "Goldilocks and the Three Bears" or "The Pot That Bubbled Over" as the cereal stirred in the bubbling pot or cooled off. How we parents view things is quickly absorbed by our children.

---

[1]*Note.* The label for Spoon Size Shredded Wheat was reprinted with permission from Nabisco Brands, Inc., Grocery Products Division, East Hanover, New Jersey.

SHREDDED WHEAT **SPOON SIZE**

100% NATURAL WHOLE WHEAT
NUTRITION INFORMATION PER SERVING

SERVING SIZE: 2/3 Cup (1 ounce; 28.3 g)
SERVINGS PER CONTAINER: 12

SPOON SIZE

Shredded Wheat Cereal	1 oz.	with 1/2 cup whole milk
Calories	110	190
Protein	3 g	7 g
Carbohydrate	23 g	29 g
Fat	1 g	5 g
Sodium	**	60 mg

**Not more than 10 mg/100 g
Not more than 10 mg/1 ounce serving

PERCENTAGE OF U.S. RECOMMENDED DAILY ALLOWANCES (U.S. RDA)

SPOON SIZE

Shredded Wheat Cereal	1 oz.	with 1/2 cup whole milk
Protein	4	15
Vitamin A	*	2
Vitamin C	*	*
Thiamine	4	8
Riboflavin	*	10
Niacin	8	8
Calcium	*	15
Iron	6	6
Phosphorus	10	20
Magnesium	8	10
Zinc	4	8
Copper	6	8

*Contains less than 2% of the U.S. RDA of these nutrients.

INGREDIENTS: 100% natural whole wheat. To help preserve the natural wheat flavor, BHT is added to the packaging material.

CARBOHYDRATE INFORMATION

SPOON SIZE Shredded Wheat

	1 OZ.	WITH 1/2 CUP WHOLE MILK
STARCH AND RELATED CARBOHYDRATES	23 g	23 g
SUCROSE AND OTHER SUGARS	0 g*	6 g
TOTAL CARBOHYDRATES	23 g	29 g

*LESS THAN 0.5 g OF NATURALLY OCCURRING SUGARS.
VALUES BY FORMULATION AND ANALYSIS.

SPOON SIZE Shredded Wheat provides 2.5% natural non-nutritive crude fiber (0.7 g per 1 ounce serving).
SPOON SIZE Shredded Wheat is ideal for LOW SODIUM DIETS, with less than 10 milligrams of naturally occurring sodium per 1 ounce serving (28.3 g).

GROCERY PRODUCTS DIVISION
EAST HANOVER, N.J. 07936
MADE IN U.S.A. © 1983 NABISCO

SUGAR YUKKIES

NUTRITION INFORMATION PER SERVING
SERVING SIZE: 1 OZ (28.4 G, ABOUT 1 CUP)
CEREAL ALONE OR WITH 1/2 CUP VITAMINS A AND D SKIM MILK OR VITAMIN D WHOLE MILK.

SERVINGS PER CONTAINER: 12.5

	CEREAL	WITH SKIM MILK	WITH WHOLE MILK
CALORIES	120	160	200
PROTEIN	1 g	5 g	5 g
CARBOHYDRATE	26 g	32 g	32 g
FAT	0 g	0 g	4 g
SODIUM	100 mg	160 mg	160 mg

PERCENTAGE OF U.S. RECOMMENDED DAILY ALLOWANCES (U.S. RDA)

PROTEIN	2	8	8
VITAMIN A	*	4	2
VITAMIN C	*	2	2
THIAMINE (VITAMIN B₁)	25	25	25
RIBOFLAVIN (VITAMIN B₂)	15	25	25
NIACIN	25	25	25
CALCIUM	*	15	15
IRON	25	25	25
VITAMIN D	*	15	15
VITAMIN B₆	25	25	25
FOLIC ACID	25	25	25
VITAMIN B₁₂	25	30	30
ZINC	15	15	15
PANTOTHENIC ACID	20	20	20

*CONTAINS LESS THAN 2 PERCENT OF THE U.S. RDA OF THESE NUTRIENTS.

INGREDIENTS: SUGAR, WHEAT FLOUR, CORN FLOUR, OAT FLOUR, RICE FLOUR, COCONUT OIL, SALT, ARTIFICIAL AND NATURAL FLAVORS, ARTIFICIAL COLORS, REDUCED IRON, NIACINAMIDE, CALCIUM PANTOTHENATE, ZINC OXIDE, THIAMINE MONONITRATE (VITAMIN B₁), BHT (A PRESERVATIVE), PYRIDOXINE HYRDOCHLORIDE (VITAMIN B₆), RIBOFLAVIN (VITAMIN B₂), FOLIC ACID AND VITAMIN B₁₂.

CARBOHYDRATE INFORMATION	1 OZ CEREAL	WITH MILK
STARCH AND RELATED CARBOHYDRATES	13 g	13 g
SUCROSE AND OTHER SUGARS	13 g	19 g
TOTAL CARBOHYDRATES	26 g	32 g

VALUES BY FORMULATION AND ANALYSIS

As you read these ideas of what foods to avoid, you may be thinking that you have just eliminated most of the foods that you and your family like. Read the next chapter and you will see that you don't have to eliminate the "fun" foods; just change certain ingredients in them to make them healthful, too.

Cooking Foods Yourself

Take an accurate count of how many times your family consumes precooked or packaged foods in 1 week. Also tally how many times you make dishes from scratch. If you are like most modern parents, you are serving packaged foods or eating out much more often than you realize. Making cooked cereal on a cold, wintry day takes about 3 extra minutes of your time, but how much extra health in your child's total lifetime will be provided by that 3 minutes per day? Telling a story while the food cooks can add to the fun for the child who is anxious to eat.

Fast Foods Aren't Always Prepackaged

For food to be prepared fast does not necessarily require that it be prepackaged or precooked. Many more women today are working mothers; they understandably seek ways to cook quickly after a busy day. Food processors, microwaves, pressure cookers, and Crockpots can enable even the busiest mom to have a dinner ready quicker than most restaurants. There are countless dishes that you can make quickly from scratch, if only you plan ahead and defrost the meat in the morning or place the main course in the oven set to automatically turn on at a certain hour and turn off again just as you arrive home from work. You don't even need to have all of the modern kitchen conveniences. Any of them and some helpful recipes, found in the final chapter of this book, can enable you to make quick, easy, delicious, and nutritious meals for the whole family.

Consider Canning, Freezing, and Joining a Co-op

Shortages of canning or freezing supplies occur from time to time. This shows that many people are aware of the benefits of "doing it yourself." People who garden save a lot on their off-season produce bills when they can or freeze. If you are new at canning or freezing, follow the directions carefully so that you don't allow any food contamination. Many companies, such as Ball canning jars, offer a complete guide to canning and freezing free or at nominal cost. Another resource is your local county extension service, which can acquaint you with numerous, valuable government bulletins.

Many communities, both large and small, are finding that food cooperatives can provide families with fresh produce at reduced costs the year round. Some cooperatives require that members work for the co-op (by driving to get produce, selling, or helping with bookkeeping), whereas other co-ops simply charge membership fees.

Whatever well-balanced meal you serve the whole family can be quickly served to your baby. Using your own foods (with no added salts or sugars), just make a few quick turns on your baby food processor, and her meal is ready.

We realize that most of our readers will still occasionally use prepared foods, but we hope that you become cognizant of how many times you use them, then cut down on them.

Offering Low-Sugar and Low-Calorie Delights

Offer a variety of foods to your child. Studies show that food preferences of young children grow directly from frequency of exposure and the opportunity to become familiar with a number of foods (Williams, 1985). An advantage of a preschool situation is that your child will often try new food items that she might not try at home due to peer pressure or to please the teacher. Remember, variety is the spice of life.

At the same time, remember, as you prepare food for your child, to season lightly. Indeed, in our household we leave salt off everything (with the exception of popcorn, a family favorite for when the child is older). In addition to reducing the amount of prepared foods, reduce your child's intake of processed sugars and fatty foods; her general health, teeth, and weight control will benefit.

Variety Is the Spice of Nutrition

Modern supermarkets are truly "super" in the variety of fresh produce and protein foods they make available to you. Americans today are truly more fortunate than our ancestors and people in other places in the world today. We are so accustomed to plenitude that we often take it for granted. Do you ever go through the grocery aisles and think twice about spending a dollar for fresh grapes, then turn to the next aisle and spend the same amount on chips? With modern refrigeration we can take advantage of the best of both worlds of food preparation: We have fresh foods readily available even in the coldest weather, yet can follow some of the tried-and-true methods of canning and freezing from the past.

Reduce Sugar in Recipes

It seems that cookies are a part of childhood, but you can choose between a cookie recipe that calls for over 3 cups of sugar or another that calls for only 1 cup of sugar. Popsicles are musts as summertime coolers. Take a few extra minutes to make your own with real fruit juices (apple, orange, grape, etc.) rather than using the sugar- and additive-laden store variety. Homemade popsicles are delicious (really fruity), fun to eat, and good for your child. Look for store-bought low-cal fruit popsicles or yogurt pops when your time is short.

Provide Naturally Sweet Treats

We keep old-fashioned, glass candy jars out on open display on our kitchen counter. They are kept temptingly full of nature's sweet snacking treats: raisins and other dried fruits (a food dehydrator can provide plenty of these at a lower price), sunflower seeds, peanuts, and other nuts the family likes. A family fun time in the evening can be centered around a bowl of popcorn, a much lower-calorie treat than chips and pretzels. If anyone in the family is really watching how many calories he or she consumes, we eliminate the butter. In any case, it is never put on in more than tiny amounts.

Use Sugarless Products

Older children have become acquainted with candy and gum in the the world outside our home. Knowing how they enjoy them we keep a very limited supply of sugarless gum and sugarless candy in the cupboard—out of sight (what they don't see they won't want). The point is that you do not need to completely eliminate snacking or the fun of food. Instead, simply modify what you offer to make it nutritious. Look in chapter 8 for ideas about nutritional, fun foods.

Serve Food With Style

At a summer staff party, our centerpiece attracted a good deal of attention. From a distance it appeared to be a gorgeous floral arrangement. Upon closer inspection, guests were delighted to find that they could eat the centerpiece. Ferns provided the foliage; the "flowers" were created from fancifully cut radishes, carrots, cherry tomatoes, olives, cauliflower florets, tiny onions, and peppers. All these were anchored with giant toothpicks or skewers. A low-cal dip (see the recipes on pages 165-167) kept guests coming back for more all afternoon.

A similar food centerpiece can be constructed with fresh fruit. Take a large head of lettuce (or for economy's sake, cover a large styrofoam ball with lettuce leaves and use the remainder of the lettuce at another time), then skewer pieces of fresh fruit in place on it with giant toothpicks.

What you eat is important, and serving it in an exciting way can really add to the food's appeal. This can be easily achieved with everyday foods as well as party foods. Take the time to set the table nicely: Add placemats, a pretty centerpiece, imaginatively folded napkins. What you serve then becomes all the more special.

Turn an everyday food item into something special. Our children love sandwiches cut into unusual shapes with a knife or cookie cutters. Turn an everyday cheese sandwich into a sunny smile. See the recipes in the next chapter for complete details on this and many other ways to turn good foods into fun foods.

Concluding Tips for Parents and Educators

Let us summarize this part of the book by referring to the words of Alvin N. Eden, M.D., noted professor of medicine, in *Trim Talk* (1978).

> The diet of most American youngsters is awful, and parents must do something about it. While there is no shortage of food, our diets grow steadily worse. Our meals are far too high in calories, fats, carbohydrates, protein, salt, and sugar.
>
> We are raising a generation of children who are often too fat while at the same time actually malnourished. Further, our children are being started on the road to hardening of the arteries and arteriosclerotic heart disease. (p. 136)

Dr. Eden lists these tips for parents:

- A wide variety of foods is necessary to provide everything a growing body requires.
- If your child is brought up eating three well-balanced meals each day and has proper eating habits, the chances are he will never become fat.

- Eating healthfully is a learned skill. Parents must teach their children what to eat, making eating habits so ingrained that they will continue the rest of their lives.
- "Fat-proof" your house. Get rid of the foods with no nutritional value and substitute a supply of healthy snacks.
- Serve a prudent diet to the whole family, low in fat and cholesterol. The entire family must work together.
- Cut down on salt. The evidence is clear that one of the main causes of high blood pressure is too much salt in the diet.
- Don't add excessive amounts of sugar to your child's food. All you accomplish by doing this is giving your child unneeded calories. Excess sugar can also lead to the problem of severe dental decay.

Chapter 8

Recipes and Preparation Activities for Parents and Children

Several years ago we began teaching nutrition in schools and found that one of the best ways for children to learn was to actively involve their parents. One popular activity evolved into this recipe section. Every February 1st we wrote a letter to parents of the school children, asking them to submit a recipe for our *Heart Health Month* Recipe Book. Each recipe had to be for a dish that was "nutritionally good" but also one that their child or family enjoyed eating. In the letter we also defined what "nutritionally good" encompassed.

Through several years we gathered hundreds of family-tested recipes, most of which were low in sugar, low in salt, made from natural ingredients, or from one of the four basic food groups. All of the recipes submitted fit the criterion of appealing to the child. Parents enthusiastically helped with gathering recipes, typing them, running them off, and collating them into a booklet.

117

We called the family recipe booklet *From Our Hearts, For Your Heart*. It was compiled and given on February 14 as a family gift to the children of the class or school participating. It was a valentine that would truly help their hearts for years to come. We always published every family's submission, for we considered how being excluded would affect their sensitive hearts.

Still, we wanted the recipes included here to be the most nutritionally sound. Therefore, Dale Wilson, a registered dietician and a mother, gleaned from the hundreds of recipes the most nutritious ones using information from Pennington and Church (1985) and the United States Department of Agriculture (1975) (see Suggested Readings list). She selected several from each food group as well as some specialty types such as snacks and foods for children on the go (for traveling, lunch boxes, or picnics). With each recipe, we included important nutritional information to help you plan your child's menu. Thus, the amounts of calories, proteins, carbohydrates, fats, cholesterol, and sodium are listed for each serving of a recipe.

Your whole family will enjoy the variety of recipes that you will find in the following sections:

1. Breads and cereals
2. Fruits and vegetables
3. Milk and dairy products
4. Poultry, fish, meat, nuts, and beans
5. Healthy snack foods
6. Foods for kids on the go

Breads and Cereals

The bread and cereal group is important because it supplies the body with carbohydrates, thiamin, niacin, and iron. Whole grain breads and cereals provide the dietary fiber that refined breads and cereals do not. Be sure to include some whole grains daily. Read labels carefully to be sure the type of flour is *whole* wheat flour. "Flour", "wheat flour," and even "unbleached wheat flour" are still white flours that may be colored to look brown.

Foods in this group include all products that are made with whole grain or enriched flour, cornmeal, and rice. Thus, all breads, muffins, hot and cold cereals, pancakes, rice, and enriched noodles are included in this group.

Growing children need four servings from this food group daily.

PEANUT BUTTER MUFFINS

2 cups sifted flour*
½ cup sugar
2½ teaspoons baking powder
½ cup chunky peanut butter
2 tablespoons corn-oil margarine
1 cup low-fat milk
2 eggs, well beaten

1. Combine dry ingredients.
2. Cut in peanut butter and margarine until mixture resembles coarse crumbs.
3. Add milk and eggs, stirring just until dry ingredients are moistened.
4. Fill greased muffin tins ⅔ full.
5. Bake at 400° for 15-17 minutes.

Yield: 18 muffins

Nutrition Information per Serving		
Calories	133	
Protein	4.4	g
Carbohydrate	17	g
Fat	5	g
Cholesterol	31	mg
Sodium	126	mg

---

*Use half white flour and half whole wheat flour to increase fiber content.

EASY BRAN MUFFINS

This batter can be made ahead and kept in the refrigerator for up to 6 weeks.

15-ounce box raisin bran cereal
2½ cups all-purpose flour
2½ cups whole wheat flour
2 cups sugar
5 teaspoons baking soda
2 teaspoons salt
4 eggs
1 cup safflower or corn oil
1 quart buttermilk

1. Combine dry ingredients. Mix well.
2. Blend the eggs, oil, and buttermilk. Add to dry ingredients. Mix well.
3. Store in airtight container in refrigerator until you are ready to bake muffins.
4. To bake muffins, oil muffin tins with safflower or corn oil or use paper muffin cups.
5. Fill muffin tin ⅔ full with mix.
6. Bake at 375° for 20 minutes.

Yield: 50 large muffins

Nutrition Information per Serving

Calories	145	
Protein	3	g
Carbohydrate	24	g
Fat	5.5	g
Cholesterol	23	mg
Sodium	256	mg

INDIAN MAIZE PANCAKES

½ cup whole kernel corn
1 egg
2 tablespoons corn oil
1½ cups flour
1 teaspoon sugar
1 teaspoon baking powder
½ teaspoon baking soda
½ teaspoon salt
1¼ cups buttermilk

1. Heat griddle to medium (375°).
2. Drain corn and set aside.
3. Beat egg.
4. Add oil, flour, sugar, baking powder, baking soda, and salt.
5. Gradually add buttermilk.
6. Beat until smooth.
7. Add corn.
8. Use ¼ cup batter for each pancake.

Yield: 10 pancakes

Nutrition Information per Serving		
Calories	108	
Protein	3.5	g
Carbohydrate	16	g
Fat	3	g
Cholesterol	29	mg
Sodium	286	mg

POCKET BREAD

POCKET BREAD

1 package active dry yeast
1¾ cups warm water
2 tablespoons corn oil
1 teaspoon salt
½ teaspoon sugar
3½ to 4 cups flour

1. Mix yeast, warm water, corn oil, salt, and sugar.
2. Gradually add 2 cups flour.
3. Beat on low speed for 30 seconds, scraping sides of bowl.
4. By hand, stir in enough flour to make a moderately stiff dough.
5. Place dough on a floured surface and roll until lightly covered with flour. Knead about 5 minutes, until smooth and elastic.
6. Cover. Let rise for 45 minutes.
7. Punch dough down and divide into 12 equal pieces.
8. Shape into balls and cover. Let rest for 10 minutes.
9. Roll the balls on a lightly floured surface. Press the dough out flat until a 5- to 6-inch circle is formed. Form circles by pressing in center and rolling outward (do not roll back and forth or bread will not puff).
10. Place 2 inches apart on ungreased baking sheet.
11. Cover. Let rise for 20-30 minutes.
12. Bake in 400° oven for 10-12 minutes or until puffed and brown.
13. To serve, slice partway along one side and stuff.

Yield: 12 servings

Nutrition Information per Serving		
Calories	153	
Protein	4	g
Carbohydrate	29	g
Fat	2	g
Cholesterol	0	
Sodium	215	mg

FILLINGS FOR POCKET BREAD

Here are some suggestions for filling the pocket bread. The variety is limitless. You can serve it either hot or cold.

1. Sliced chicken, turkey, ham, or roast beef with lettuce and tomato.
2. Taco filling: seasoned ground beef, chopped lettuce and tomato, cheddar cheese, and taco sauce.
3. Scrambled eggs and ham.
4. Pimento cheese spread.
5. Tuna or chicken salad.

RISE AND SHINE OATMEAL

You don't have to wait until lunch to enjoy peanut butter and jelly. Swirl it into your morning oatmeal. A real treat for kids and adults!

1½ cups quick-cooking rolled oats
⅓ cup peanut butter
⅓ cup of your favorite jelly or jam

1. Cook oats according to directions on package.
2. Pour prepared oatmeal into 4 bowls.
3. Spoon peanut butter and jelly on top of oatmeal. Stir to swirl.

Yield: 4 servings

Nutrition Information per Serving		
Calories	308	
Protein	10	g
Carbohydrate	44	g
Fat	12	g
Cholesterol	0	
Sodium	343	mg

FILLINGS FOR POCKET BREAD

RISE AND SHINE OATMEAL

CORNY CORN BREAD

CORNY CORN BREAD

12-ounce can whole kernel corn with sweet peppers
1 cup yellow cornmeal
1 cup flour
¼ cup sugar
1 tablespoon baking powder
1 teaspoon salt
1 egg
1¼ cups skim milk
2 tablespoons corn oil

1. Grease a 9 × 9 × 2-inch baking pan with oil.
2. Drain corn.
3. Mix corn meal, flour, sugar, baking powder, and salt into bowl.
4. Add eggs, milk, oil, and corn. Stir until well blended.
5. Pour into pan. Bake at 425° for 35-40 minutes.
6. Cut into 9 squares and serve warm.

Yield: 9 servings

Nutrition Information per Serving		
Calories	190	
Protein	5	g
Carbohydrate	34	g
Fat	10	g
Cholesterol	31	mg
Sodium	494	mg

FRENCH TOAST

4 slices whole wheat bread
2 eggs
½ cup skim milk
Dash cinnamon
3 tablespoons corn-oil margarine

1. In a mixing bowl, mix eggs, milk, and cinnamon. Pour into pie plate.
2. In a skillet, melt ¼ of margarine (or use a nonstick spray, such as Pam, to reduce fats).
3. Dip bread in egg mixture and place in skillet.
4. Brown bread on both sides.
5. Serve hot with honey or syrup.

Yield: 4 servings

Nutrition Information per Serving		
Calories	202	
Protein	6.5	g
Carbohydrate	13	g
Fat	14	g
Cholesterol	138	mg
Sodium	209	mg

BAKED CHEESE GRITS

A new twist to grits. Kids love cheese, so they'll be sure to love this combo!

2 cups water
¼ teaspoon salt
½ cup quick-cooking grits, uncooked
½ cup (2 ounces) shredded cheddar cheese
1 egg
¼ cup skim milk
¼ teaspoon pepper
⅛ teaspoon Worcestershire sauce
Vegetable cooking spray

1. Bring water and salt to a boil in a saucepan.
2. Stir in grits. Cover and reduce heat to low.
3. Cook for 5 minutes until grits are done.
4. Combine grits with next 5 ingredients. Mix well.
5. Pour into 1 quart baking dish that has been sprayed with cooking spray.
6. Bake at 350° for 40 minutes.

Yield: 6 servings

Nutrition Information per Serving		
Calories	104	
Protein	5	g
Carbohydrate	11	g
Fat	4.25	g
Cholesterol	56	mg
Sodium	172	mg

☆

BIRDSEED BREAD

2 cups Bisquick baking mix
½ cup cold water
¼ teaspoon garlic powder
¼ cup corn-oil margarine
2 tablespoons sesame seeds
2 tablespoons salted sunflower seeds

1. Preheat oven to 425°.
2. Mix baking mix, water, and garlic powder.
3. On an ungreased cookie sheet, pat the dough into a 10-inch circle.
4. Melt the margarine and brush the dough with it.
5. Sprinkle sesame seeds and sunflower seeds on top of dough.
6. Gently press seeds into dough, using a rubber spatula.
7. Cut circle into 12 equal pieces (pie-shaped).
8. Bake 15-20 minutes or until golden brown.
9. Serve warm. Bread will break into wedges.

Yield: 12 servings

Nutrition Information per Serving		
Calories	169	
Protein	2	g
Carbohydrate	13	g
Fat	12	g
Cholesterol	0	
Sodium	322	mg

GETALONG GRANOLA

GETALONG GRANOLA

6 cups rolled oats
1 cup powdered non-fat dry milk
1 cup wheat germ
1 cup bran
1½ cups mixed nuts
1 cup sunflower seeds
1 cup honey
½ cup sunflower or safflower oil
2 teaspoons vanilla
1 cup raisins

1. Mix first 6 ingredients.
2. Mix honey, oil, and vanilla. Pour over granola mixture. Stir until well-blended.
3. Spread mixture onto a jelly roll pan.
4. Bake at 250° for 2½ hours. Stir mixture every 30 minutes.
5. Add raisins to mixture during the last 30 minutes of baking time.
6. Cool and store in airtight container.

Yield: 24 (½ cup) servings

Nutrition Information per Serving		
Calories	299	
Protein	9	g
Carbohydrate	38	g
Fat	14	g
Cholesterol	trace	
Sodium	38	mg

☆

MULTIGRAIN PIZZA CRUST

A different sort of pizza crust! Top it with your favorite pizza sauce and toppings. Be sure to let the kids help assemble the pizza.

1 cup regular or quick-cooking oats
½ cup all-purpose flour
½ cup whole wheat flour
⅓ cup yellow cornmeal
1 teaspoon baking powder
⅔ cup skim milk
¼ cup safflower or corn oil
Your favorite toppings, sauce, and cheese

1. Place oats in a blender; cover and blend until a flour is formed.
2. Sift together dry ingredients.
3. Add milk and oil. Mix well.
4. Knead gently on a lightly floured surface, approximately 10-15 strokes.
5. Press into a greased 12-inch pizza pan.
6. Bake at 425° for 12 minutes or until brown.
7. Add your favorite toppings and return pizza to oven for 10 to 15 minutes.

Yield: 6 servings

Nutrition Information per Serving (Crust Only)		
Calories	259	
Protein	7	g
Carbohydrate	35	g
Fat	8	g
Cholesterol	trace	
Sodium	87	mg

WHOLE WHEAT ANIMAL CRACKERS

You can make traditional square crackers or be creative and let your children help make "animal" crackers with their favorite cookie cutters!

⅓ cup shortening
⅓ cup skim milk
2 tablespoons honey
1 cup whole wheat flour
⅔ cup all-purpose flour
3 tablespoons yellow cornmeal
2 tablespoons wheat germ
½ teaspoon baking powder
¼ teaspoon salt

1. Preheat oven to 350°.
2. Mix shortening, milk, and honey in 2-quart bowl.
3. Stir in remaining ingredients until blended well.
4. Divide dough into halves. Roll out ⅟₁₆ inch thick on lightly floured surface.
5. Cut with animal-shaped cookie cutters.
6. Place on ungreased cookie sheets.
7. Bake until edges are very light brown, approximately 8-10 minutes.

Yield: 8 dozen crackers

Nutrition Information per Serving (6 crackers)		
Calories	95	
Protein	2	g
Carbohydrate	13	g
Fat	4.3	g
Cholesterol	0	
Sodium	64	mg

WHOLE WHEAT BREAD

1 package active dry yeast
1¼ cups warm water
2 cups all-purpose flour
¼ cup honey
2 tablespoons safflower oil
1½ teaspoons salt
1¾ to 2¼ cups whole wheat flour

1. Dissolve yeast in warm water.
2. Add flour, honey, oil, and salt. Beat on low speed until moist, then beat on medium speed for 4 minutes.
3. Stir in enough whole wheat flour to make dough easy to handle.
4. Place dough on a floured surface and roll until lightly covered with flour.
5. Knead until smooth and elastic, about 5 minutes.
6. Place in greased bowl; turn greased side up.
7. Cover and let rise until dough doubles, about 1 hour.
8. Punch down dough, roll into rectangle 18 × 9 inches. Roll dough up tightly and place in a 9 × 5 × 3-inch loaf pan.
9. Brush with margarine and sprinkle with whole wheat flour or crushed rolled oats, or wheat germ or wheat bran.
10. Let rise until dough doubles, about 1 hour.
11. Bake at 375° for 40-45 minutes.

Yield:　1 loaf (20 slices)

Nutrition Information per Serving		
Calories	105	
Protein	3	g
Carbohydrate	21	g
Fat	2	g
Cholesterol	0	
Sodium	174	mg

Remember that when making your favorite bread, you can alter the recipe to make it lower in sugar, higher in fiber, or lower in salt. You can reduce the salt and sugar in the recipe by ⅓ to ½. You can increase the fiber by adding 2-3 tablespoons wheat germ, oat bran, or wheat bran. These changes can enhance the nutritional value without changing the taste.

WHOLE WHEAT SOFT PRETZELS

1 package active dry yeast
1½ cups warm water (105° to 115°)
2¾ cups all-purpose flour
3 teaspoons sugar
½ teaspoon salt
1 to 1½ cups whole wheat flour
1 egg
1 tablespoon cold water
2 tablespoons coarse salt

1. Dissolve yeast in warm water.
2. Add all-purpose flour, sugar, and the ½ teaspoon of salt. Mix well with mixer, beating on medium speed.
3. Stir in enough whole wheat flour to make dough easy to handle.
4. Turn dough onto lightly floured surface. Knead until smooth and elastic, about 5-7 minutes.
5. Place in greased bowl, turn greased side up.
6. Cover. Let rise in warm place until dough doubles, about 1 hour.
7. Preheat oven to 475°.
8. Punch dough down, divide in half. Divide each half into 6 equal pieces.
9. Roll each piece into a rope 15 inches long.
10. Place rope on a greased cookie sheet. Bring left end of rope over the middle of rope to form a loop. Bring the right end of rope up and over the first loop to form a pretzel shape.
11. Place pretzels about 3 inches apart on baking sheet.
12. Mix egg and cold water. Brush pretzels with mixture and sprinkle with coarse salt.

13. Bake for 15-20 minutes or until brown.
14. Serve with mustard!

Yield: 12 servings

Nutrition Information per Serving		
Calories	154	
Protein	5.4	g
Carbohydrate	32	g
Fat	1	g
Cholesterol	23	mg
Sodium	1,253	mg*

---

*To reduce the sodium content, leave off the coarse salt. This will reduce the sodium content to only 103 mg.

ABC PANCAKES

ABC PANCAKES

½ cup all-purpose flour
¾ cup whole wheat flour
½ teaspoon baking soda
1 tablespoon sugar
½ teaspoon salt
1 egg
1 cup buttermilk
1 tablespoon corn or safflower oil

1. Sift dry ingredients together.
2. Combine egg, buttermilk, and oil. Add dry ingredients. Stir well until moist. The batter will still be lumpy.
3. Pour batter onto a hot griddle, using ⅓ to ½ cup batter. This is when ABC fun begins: Form pancakes into shapes that will delight your child, such as letters, numbers, faces, animal shapes, and so on.
4. Cook on both sides. Serve hot.

Yield: 8 pancakes

Nutrition Information per Serving		
Calories	106	
Protein	4	g
Carbohydrate	16	g
Fat	3	g
Cholesterol	35	mg
Sodium	212	mg

JELLY-IN-THE-BELLY MUFFINS

This muffin has a surprise of gooey jelly in the middle.

1 cup all-purpose flour
1 cup whole wheat flour
⅓ cup brown sugar
2 teaspoons baking powder
¼ teaspoon baking soda
½ teaspoon salt
1 egg
1 cup buttermilk
3 tablespoons safflower or corn oil
¼ cup chopped pecans
4 tablespoons of your favorite jam or jelly*

1. Mix flours, brown sugar, baking powder, baking soda and salt in a large mixing bowl. Make a well in the center.
2. Stir together the egg, buttermilk, and oil in a small bowl.
3. Add mixture to dry ingredients. Stir just until moist.
4. Add pecans and fold in gently.
5. Place 2 tablespoons batter into each muffin cup.
6. Place 1 teaspoon jam or jelly on top of batter.
7. Top with remaining batter, dividing it evenly among 12 muffins.
8. Bake in a 400° oven for 20-25 minutes.
9. Serve warm.

Yield: 12 muffins

Nutrition Information per Serving		
Calories	170	
Protein	4	g
Carbohydrate	28	g
Fat	5	g
Cholesterol	24	mg
Sodium	215	mg

*Try the low-sugar, low-calorie jellies.

Fruits and Vegetables

The fruit and vegetable group is important because it provides vitamins A and C, carbohydrates, fiber, and other vitamins and minerals. No one single food provides all the nutrients the body needs, so it is important to vary the fruits and vegetables that you offer your child. This helps assure that you will meet your child's daily needs. This group contains a wide variety to choose from, so teach your child early on to take advantage of the assortment.

A serving size is ½ cup of cooked vegetables or fruits or 1 cup raw vegetables or fruits. Four servings a day are recommended for growing children. Dark green, leafy, or yellow vegetables and fruits are recommended three or four times weekly for vitamin A. Citrus fruit is recommended daily for vitamin C.

FRIENDLY DOG SALAD

1 pear half (unsweetened if canned)
1 pitted prune
2 orange slices
1 maraschino cherry
2 raisins
1 lettuce leaf

1. Place washed lettuce leaf on small plate.
2. Place pear half cut side down on lettuce leaf.
3. Cut prune in half. Place halves on sides of pear for ears.
4. Scoop out tiny holes for the eyes. Place the raisins in the holes.
5. Place the cherry for the nose.
6. Arrange the orange slices for the collar.

Yield: 1 serving

Nutrition Information per Serving	
Calories	80
Protein	0.75 g
Carbohydrate	22 g
Fat	0.5 g
Cholesterol	0
Sodium	1.5 mg

FRIENDLY DOG SALAD

FRUIT CUP SUPREME
IN A WATERMELON BOAT

1 watermelon
2 cups fresh pineapple, cut in chunks
2 cups cantaloupe balls
2 cups honeydew melon balls
2 cups strawberries, sliced

1. Cut watermelon in half lengthwise, and scoop out fruit. Reserve 2 cups pieces or balls for the salad.
2. Scallop the watermelon edge to make attractive.
3. Mix the fresh fruits.
4. Ladle into melon "boat" and chill.

Let the kids help you cut up the fruit. They love to make melon balls!

Yield: 20 servings (½ cup each)

Nutrition Information per Serving	
Calories	29
Protein	0.5 g
Carbohydrate	7 g
Fat	0.2 g
Cholesterol	0
Sodium	4 mg

POPCORN BANANA SALAD

POPCORN BANANA SALAD

1 medium banana
2 lettuce leaves
2 tablespoons low-calorie mayonnaise or yogurt-type dressing
2 tablespoons popped popcorn

1. Place lettuce leaves on plate.
2. Cut banana in half lengthwise and place on lettuce leaves.
3. Cover with mayonnaise or yogurt-type dressing.
4. Sprinkle with popcorn.

Yield: 1 serving

Nutrition Information per Serving		
Calories	230	
Protein	1.6	g
Carbohydrate	33	g
Fat	12	g
Cholesterol	0	
Sodium	219	mg

VEGETABLE BOUQUETS

1 cup broccoli flowerets
1 cup cauliflower flowerets
1 medium carrot, cut into strips
½ cup Italian dressing

1. Place vegetables in a large plastic bag.
2. Pour Italian dressing over vegetables.
3. Place bag in mixing bowl.
4. Cover and chill at least 2 hours, turning bag occasionally to coat vegetables.
5. To serve, drain vegetables and arrange in four small vases or custard cups to resemble bouquets.

Yield: 4 servings

Nutrition Information per Serving		
Calories	163	
Protein	2	g
Carbohydrate	8	g
Fat	14	g
Cholesterol	0	
Sodium	240	mg

STUFFED POTATOES

STUFFED POTATOES

2 medium baking potatoes
1 cup low-fat cottage cheese
2 teaspoons chives
1 teaspoon onion powder
Paprika

1. Preheat oven to 425°.
2. Bake potatoes until done.
3. Cut potatoes in half lengthwise and scoop out insides.
4. Return potato shells to oven and bake until crisp.
5. Whip potato insides with remaining ingredients (except paprika).
6. Place mixture back in potato skins.
7. Sprinkle with paprika.
8. Bake until heated through.

Yield: 4 servings

Nutrition Information per Serving		
Calories	92	
Protein	8	g
Carbohydrate	13	g
Fat	0.6	g
Cholesterol	2.5	mg
Sodium	232	mg

CARROT RAISIN SALAD

3 cups grated carrots
¾ cup raisins
⅓ cup low-calorie mayonnaise
1 teaspoon sugar
2 tablespoons evaporated skim milk, undiluted
1 tablespoon lemon juice

1. Combine carrots and raisins in bowl.
2. Mix the remaining ingredients separately.
3. Toss with the carrots and raisins.
4. Chill in refrigerator prior to serving.

Yield:　6 servings

Nutrition Information per Serving		
Calories	125	
Protein	2	g
Carbohydrate	22	g
Fat	5	g
Cholesterol	5	mg
Sodium	111	mg

CARROT RAISIN SALAD

HOMEMADE APPLESAUCE

5 cooking apples
½ cup water
2 sticks cinnamon
3 tablespoons sugar

1. Peel and core apples and cut into pieces.
2. Place apples into saucepan and add water and cinnamon.
3. Cook until apples are tender and mash easily.
4. Remove cinnamon sticks and throw away.
5. Mash apples with potato masher.
6. Add sugar.
7. Serve warm or cold.

Yield: 4 servings

Nutrition Information per Serving		
Calories	136	
Protein	trace	
Carbohydrate	35	g
Fat	0.5	g
Cholesterol	0	
Sodium	1	mg

VOLCANO SALAD

1 medium head of lettuce
½ cantaloupe
1 pound cooked lean ham
8 ounces cheddar cheese
4 strawberries
⅓ cup salad dressing
2 tablespoons chili sauce
⅛ teaspoon oregano

1. Clean lettuce thoroughly. Reserve eight large leaves. Tear rest into bite-sized chunks.
2. Place two leaves each in four salad bowls.
3. Mound up lettuce pieces in center of lettuce leaves.
4. Hold lettuce into place with thinly sliced cantaloupe slices.
5. Cut ham and cheddar cheese into 4 × ½-inch strips.
6. Place four or five strips of ham and cheese around each mound to look like sides of a volcano.
7. Prepare Lava Dressing by mixing salad dressing, chili sauce, and oregano.
8. Top each salad with a spoonful of Lava Dressing.
9. Place a strawberry on top of each salad as volcano's fire.

Yield: 4 servings

Nutrition Information per Serving		
Calories	537	
Protein	50	g
Carbohydrate	11.5	g
Fat	32	g
Cholesterol	60	mg
Sodium	1,775	mg

BANANA FRITTERS

BANANA FRITTERS

2 cups cornflake crumbs
1 tablespoon sugar
6 ripe bananas, peeled
⅓ cup orange juice
2 tablespoons corn-oil margarine

1. Combine crumbs and sugar.
2. Cut bananas in half lengthwise and dip in orange juice.
3. Roll banana in cornflake crumbs.
4. Place bananas on cookie sheet that has been sprayed with vegetable cooking spray.
5. Melt margarine and drizzle over bananas.
6. Bake in a 400° oven until brown.

Yield: 6 servings

Nutrition Information per Serving

Calories	185	
Protein	2	g
Carbohydrate	37	g
Fat	4.4	g
Cholesterol	0	
Sodium	147	mg

☆

COOKED CARROTS AND PINEAPPLE

Carrots are an excellent source of vitamin A. Combining the carrots with pineapple gives them a unique flavor.

4 large carrots
16-ounce can pineapple chunks (no sugar added)
¼ teaspoon salt
1 teaspoon cornstarch
1 teaspoon corn-oil margarine

1. Wash and slice carrots.
2. Drain pineapple and place juice in saucepan.
3. Add carrots, margarine, and salt. Cook until tender.
4. Add pineapple chunks.
5. Mix cornstarch with small amount of water.
6. Stir cornstarch into carrot mixture. Cook until thickened.

Yield: 4 servings

Nutrition Information per Serving

Calories	92
Protein	1.4 g
Carbohydrate	20 g
Fat	1.5 g
Cholesterol	0
Sodium	202 mg

☆

HOBO VEGETABLES

Having a backyard cookout? Try this easy way to cook the vegetables for the meal.

4 carrots, peeled and cut in thirds
4 potatoes, cut in wedges
4 onions, peeled and cut in half
4 tablespoons corn-oil margarine
Black pepper to taste

1. Cut four pieces of heavy-duty aluminum foil.
2. Place carrots, potatoes, and onions in the center of the foil.
3. Add 1 tablespoon margarine to each. Use pepper as desired.
4. Close snugly and seal.
5. Place over hot coals for 45-60 minutes, turning occasionally.

Yield: 4 servings

Nutrition Information per Serving

Calories	259	
Protein	5	g
Carbohydrate	36	g
Fat	12	g
Cholesterol	0	
Sodium	189	mg

☆

OVEN FRENCH FRIES

French fries without frying! They are lower in calories and fat than the traditional fried type.

4 medium potatoes (Irish potatoes are a good choice)
1-2 tablespoons corn or safflower oil

1. Peel potatoes and cut into long strips. Dry strips thoroughly with paper towels.
2. Toss potato strips with oil in a bowl.
3. When strips are thoroughly coated with oil, spread them on a cookie sheet.
4. Bake at 475° for 30-35 minutes. Turn potatoes occasionally to brown on all sides. If crisper potatoes are desired, place under the broiler for 1-2 minutes.

Yield: 6 servings

Nutrition Information per Serving	
Calories	91
Protein	1.4 g
Carbohydrate	11 g
Fat	4.6 g
Cholesterol	0
Sodium	0*

*Sodium content is 0 if you leave the salt shaker alone. Remember that a teaspoon of salt contains 2,300 mg of sodium.

OVEN FRENCH FRIES

WALDORF SALAD

WALDORF SALAD

2 cups diced unpeeled apples
½ cup diced celery
¼ cup chopped walnuts
½ cup raisins
1 teaspoon lemon juice
½ cup low-calorie mayonnaise

1. Combine above ingredients. Mix well.
2. Chill well before serving.

Yield: 6 servings

Nutrition Information per Serving		
Calories	186	
Protein	1.5	g
Carbohydrate	27	g
Fat	10	g
Cholesterol	7	mg
Sodium	131	mg

SMALL-FRY VEGETABLE STIR FRY

Select a variety of vegetables to use in this stir-fry dish. There are hundreds of possibilities. Use your child's favorites. Let him help make the selection.

2 pounds assorted fresh vegetables: broccoli, onions, cauliflower, carrots, mushrooms, squash, tomatoes, snow peas, green peppers, celery, and so on.
1 tablespoon corn-oil margarine
1 tablespoon corn or safflower oil
2 tablespoons broth
1 teaspoon soy sauce
½ teaspoon pepper

1. Wash vegetables and cut into bite-size pieces.
2. Heat the margarine and oil in a large skillet or wok.
3. Add the vegetables and broth. Cook until tender-crisp, stirring mixture frequently. Cooking time is approximately 5 minutes.
4. Add soy sauce and pepper. Mix well.
5. Serve warm.

Yield: 6 servings

Nutrition Information per Serving		
Calories	90	
Protein	4	g
Carbohydrate	11	g
Fat	5	g
Cholestrol	0	
Sodium	139	mg

SMALL-FRY VEGETABLE STIR FRY

FRUIT DELIGHT

FRUIT DELIGHT

1 apple, diced
2 oranges, peeled and sectioned
1 grapefruit, peeled and sectioned
½ cup raisins
½ cup walnuts, chopped
½ cup shredded coconut
½ cup rolled oats
½ cup maple syrup
¼ cup pumpkin seeds

Combine ingredients and mix well.

Yield: 10 servings (½ cup each)

Nutrition Information per Serving		
Calories	195	
Protein	4	g
Carbohydrate	28.75	g
Fat	8.5	g
Cholestrol	0	
Sodium	5	mg

Milk and Dairy Products

The milk group is important because it provides protein, calcium, phosphorus, riboflavin, and vitamins A and D. This group includes the many varieties of milk (skim, lowfat, whole, buttermilk) and a variety of milk products, such as cheese, yogurt, and cottage cheese.

The recommended number of servings per day:

Children under 9 years	2-3 servings
Children 9-12 years	3 servings
Teens	4 servings
Adults	2 servings

A serving equals 1 cup of milk or yogurt or 1¼ ounces of cheese. Remember that milk need not be your only choice. You can include some of the many varieties of milk products to meet the daily requirements of your child and yourself.

CHOCOLATE MILKSHAKES

A lower fat version of the traditional shake!

¾ cup skim milk
3 tablespoons chocolate-flavored syrup
2 cups vanilla ice milk

1. Pour milk and chocolate syrup into blender and mix well.
2. Add ice milk and blend just until smooth.
3. Serve immediately.

Yield: 2 servings

Nutrition Information per Serving		
Calories	271	
Protein	9	g
Carbohydrate	46	g
Fat	6	g
Cholesterol	20	mg
Sodium	167	mg

CHOCOLATE MILKSHAKES

GARDEN PATCH CHEESE AND MACARONI

1 cup tricolor elbow macaroni
2 tablespoons corn-oil margarine
2 tablespoons all-purpose flour
Dash pepper
1 cup skim milk
1 cup (4 ounces) cubed American, cheddar, and/or mozzarella cheese
1 pound package frozen mixed vegetables

1. Cook macaroni according to direction on package. Drain.
2. Prepare sauce. Melt margarine in a medium saucepan.
3. Stir in flour and pepper. Add milk.
4. Cook and stir until mixture thickens.
5. Add cheese. Stir until cheese melts.
6. Mix together cooked pasta, sauce, and frozen vegetables.
7. Place in 1-quart casserole.
8. Bake at 350° for 20-25 minutes.

Yield: 4 servings

Nutrition Information per Serving		
Calories	447	
Protein	19	g
Carbohydrate	56	g
Fat	16	g
Cholesterol	31	mg
Sodium	308	mg

PURPLE COWS

While I was growing up, my grandmother used to recite poems to me. One of her favorites was a poem about a purple cow. It went like this:

Purple Cow
by Gelett Burgess

I've never seen a purple cow,
I never hope to see one.
But I can tell you, anyhow,
I'd rather see than be one.

2 cups vanilla ice milk
6-ounce can frozen grape juice concentrate
1½ cups skim milk

1. Place ingredients in blender.
2. Blend until smooth.
3. Serve immediately.

Yield: 4 servings

Nutrition Information per Serving		
Calories	196	
Protein	6.5	g
Carbohydrate	40	g
Fat	3	g
Cholesterol	10.5	mg
Sodium	104	mg

CHEESE TOAST

CHEESE TOAST

Quick and easy!

1 slice whole wheat bread
1 ounce cheddar or American cheese

1. Place cheese on top of bread.
2. Broil in oven until cheese melts.

Try a low-fat cheese, such as part-skim mozzarella, instead of the traditional cheddar or American cheese.

Yield: 1 serving

Nutrition Information per Serving		
Calories	175	
Protein	9.5	g
Carbohydrate	12	g
Fat	10.5	g
Cholesterol	30	mg
Sodium	335	mg

CHEESE FONDUE

11-ounce can cheddar cheese soup (undiluted)
½ teaspoon Worcestershire sauce
Bread cubes and/or assorted vegetables (carrots, celery, peppers, cauliflower, cucumbers, broccoli buds, etc.)

1. Mix cheddar cheese soup and Worcestershire sauce. Heat for 5 minutes.
2. Serve with bread cubes or assorted vegetables. Let your child choose his favorite vegetables or take this as a time to introduce him to new ones.

Yield: 6 servings

Nutrition Information per Serving		
Calories	52	
Protein	2	g
Carbohydrate	4	g
Fat	3.5	g
Cholesterol	10	mg
Sodium	324	mg

PEANUT BUTTER SHAKE

PEANUT BUTTER SHAKE

2 cups cold skim milk
⅓ cup creamy peanut butter
2 tablespoons honey
1 banana, sliced
6-8 crushed ice cubes

1. Place all ingredients in blender except ice cubes.
2. Blend on low speed.
3. Add crushed ice cubes.
4. Blend slowly again until smooth.

Yield: 3 servings

Nutrition Information per Serving		
Calories	285	
Protein	13	g
Carbohydrate	39	g
Fat	13	g
Cholesterol	2.6	mg
Sodium	117.8	mg

BEEF AND CHEESE LOG

1 tablespoon low-calorie salad dressing (mayonnaise or yogurt type)
3-ounce package softened cream cheese
1 cup sharp cheddar cheese, grated
3-ounce package chopped pressed beef
½ cup pecans, finely chopped

1. Mix dressing with softened cream cheese.
2. Add cheddar cheese and beef. Mix well.
3. Shape into log.
4. Roll in pecans and wrap in wax paper.
5. Chill in refrigerator.
6. Serve with wheat or other whole grain crackers.

Yield: 8 servings

Nutrition Information per Serving		
Calories	175	
Protein	9	g
Carbohydrate	2	g
Fat	15	g
Cholesterol	27	mg
Sodium	590	mg

BEEF AND CHEESE LOG

COTTAGE CHEESE BREAD

COTTAGE CHEESE BREAD

5½ to 6 cups flour*
3 tablespoons sugar
4 teaspoons caraway seed
1 envelope yeast
1 teaspoon salt
½ cup water
2 tablespoons corn-oil margarine
2 cups (16 ounces) low-fat cottage cheese (room temperature)
1 tablespoon grated onion

1. Stir together 2 cups flour, sugar, caraway seed, yeast, and salt in a large mixing bowl. Set aside.
2. Heat water and margarine in saucepan until warm (120-130°).
3. Gradually beat water and margarine into flour mixture.
4. Add cottage cheese and onion.
5. Beat at high speed for 5 minutes.
6. Stir in enough flour to make a stiff dough.
7. Turn onto a lightly floured surface and knead for 8-10 minutes or until dough is no longer sticky.
8. Place in large greased bowl, turning dough to grease all sides.
9. Cover with plastic wrap and dish towel. Let rise in warm, draft-free place for 1 hour or until dough has doubled.
10. Punch down and knead lightly (less than 1 minute) until smooth.
11. Cut in half, and cover. Let rise 15 minutes.
12. Roll out each half into a 12 × 9-inch rectangle.
13. Starting at narrow edge, roll each half of dough into a loaf.
14. Place each loaf seam-side down, in greased 9 × 5 × 3-inch loaf pan.
15. Cover. Let rise in warm, draft-free place for 1 hour or until doubled.

---

*You may use half whole wheat flour and half white flour if desired. This would increase the fiber content.

16. Bake at 375° for 20-30 minutes or until loaves sound hollow when tapped.

17. Remove from pans and let cool.

Yield: 2 loaves (8 servings per loaf)

Nutrition Information per Serving		
Calories	203	
Protein	13	g
Carbohydrate	35.9	g
Fat	3	g
Cholesterol	2	mg
Sodium	268	mg

VANILLA FROZEN YOGURT*

1 cup sugar
2 envelopes unflavored gelatin
2 cups skim milk
5½ cups plain low-fat yogurt
4½ teaspoons vanilla extract

1. Combine sugar, gelatin, and milk in a medium saucepan. Let stand for about 2 minutes.
2. Cook over low heat, stirring constantly for 6 minutes or until gelatin and sugar dissolve. Let cool.
3. Stir in yogurt and vanilla. Chill.
4. Pour mixture into freezer can of a 1-gallon hand-turned or electric freezer. Freeze according to instructions.
5. Serve immediately or let ripen 1 hour.

Yield: 11 cups

Nutrition Information per Serving

Calories	81	
Protein	4	g
Carbohydrate	14	g
Fat	1	g
Cholesterol	4	mg
Sodium	52	mg

*Although it contains some sugar, frozen yogurt contains about 54 calories less than the same amount of ice cream. It's also lower in fat and higher in calcium.

☆

STRAWBERRY YOGURT POPSICLE

2 cartons unsweetened frozen strawberries (10 ounces each)
½ cup sugar
1 tablespoon unflavored gelatin
16 ounces plain low-fat yogurt
10 paper cups
10 wooden sticks

1. Drain strawberries, saving liquid.
2. Place liquid in saucepan, adding the sugar and gelatin.
3. Cook over low heat, stirring constantly until sugar and gelatin dissolve. Cool.
4. Mix strawberries, yogurt, and gelatin mixture in blender until smooth.
5. Pour yogurt mixture into 10 paper cups. Cover each with foil.
6. Make a slit in foil and insert stick.
7. Freeze until firm.
8. When ready to eat, run warm water over outside of cup to loosen.

Yield: 10 servings

Nutrition Information per Serving		
Calories	83	
Protein	3	g
Carbohydrate	17	g
Fat	0.75	g
Cholesterol	2.8	mg
Sodium	33	mg

STRAWBERRY YOGURT POPSICLE

ICE MILK SUNDAE

ICE MILK SUNDAE

Ice milk is lower in fat and calories than regular ice cream. Your child will love it with one of the fruit toppings!

½ cup ice milk
¼ cup fruit topping (see following recipes)

Combine ice milk and topping.

Yield: 1 serving

STRAWBERRY-BANANA TOPPING

STRAWBERRY-BANANA TOPPING

2 tablespoons cornstarch
2 cups unsweetened apple juice
2 tablespoons honey
1 cup fresh sliced strawberries
1 medium banana, sliced

1. Combine cornstarch and apple juice. Slowly stir in honey. Mix well.
2. Cook over low heat until thick, stirring constantly.
3. Remove from heat; let cool.
4. Fold in strawberries and banana.

Yield: 2½ cups

SPICY APPLE TOPPING

2 cups unsweetened apple juice, divided
1¾ cups diced apples
2 tablespoons dark brown sugar
¼ teaspoon apple pie spice
2 tablespoons cornstarch

1. Combine 1¾ cups apple juice, apples, brown sugar, and apple pie spice. Bring mixture to a boil, reduce heat, and simmer 5 to 10 minutes or until apples are tender.
2. Dissolve cornstarch in remaining ¼ cup apple juice. Stir into hot mixture.
3. Cook over medium heat, stirring constantly until mixture thickens.
4. Remove from heat; let cool.

Yield: 2½ cups

Nutrition Information per Serving			
	Ice Milk	Strawberry-Banana	Spicy Apple
Calories	92	64	61
Protein	2.6 g	trace	trace
Carbohydrate	14.5 g	16 g	15 g
Fat	2.8 g	trace	trace
Cholesterol	9 mg	0	0
Sodium	52 mg	2 mg	2 mg

FRUIT SMOOTHIE

A great drink for a child, full of calcium and vitamin C!

1 cup low-fat milk
1 medium banana (frozen for extra creaminess)
8 frozen or fresh strawberries (unsweetened)
2 tablespoons frozen orange juice concentrate (unsweetened)

Mix all ingredients in a blender and blend until smooth.

Yield: 1 serving

Nutrition Information per Serving		
Calories	299	
Protein	11	g
Carbohydrate	56	g
Fat	6	g
Cholesterol	18	mg
Sodium	126	mg

FRUIT AND YOGURT CUP

1 cup plain low-fat yogurt
½ cup fresh unsweetened fruit of your child's choice, such as bananas, mashed; strawberries, sliced or mashed; pineapple, canned, crushed, or fresh chopped; peaches, canned or fresh (chopped or mashed)

1. Mix yogurt and fruit
2. Serve cold.

Yield: 1 serving

Nutrition Information per Serving		
Calories	196	
Protein	14	g
Carbohydrate	29	g
Fat	5	g
Cholesterol	14	mg
Sodium	159	mg

YOGURT DIP

1 cup plain yogurt
½ package ranch-style dressing mix

1. Mix the yogurt and dressing mix thoroughly
2. Serve with assorted raw vegetables

Yield: 6 servings

Nutrition Information per Serving		
Calories	74	
Protein	2	g
Carbohydrate	4	g
Fat	5	g
Cholesterol	4	mg
Sodium	395	mg

COTTAGE CHEESE HERB DIP

COTTAGE CHEESE HERB DIP

1 cup low-fat cottage cheese
2 tablespoons lemon juice
2 tablespoons low-fat milk
2 tablespoons salad dressing
¼ cup coarsely chopped parsley
½ teaspoon tarragon leaves
Dash pepper

1. Mix all ingredients in blender until smooth and creamy. Chill.

2. Serve with assorted raw vegetables.

Yield: 6 servings

Nutrition Information per Serving		
Calories	61	
Protein	6	g
Carbohydrate	3.4	g
Fat	3	g
Cholesterol	4	mg
Sodium	195	mg

COTTAGE CHEESE DIP

2 tablespoons low-fat milk
12 ounces low-fat cottage cheese
¼ teaspoon garlic powder
Dash cayenne pepper
1 teaspoon onion salt*
Assorted vegetables (carrots, celery, peppers,
**   cauliflower, cucumbers, broccoli, and so on)**

1. Blend in blender first 5 ingredients until smooth, approximately 1 minute.
2. Serve with assorted crisp vegetables. Kids love to munch on veggies when they can also dip.

Yield: 6 servings (2½ tablespoons each)

Nutrition Information per Serving		
Calories	56	
Protein	8	g
Carbohydrate	2.5	g
Fat	1.3	g
Cholesterol	5.5	mg
Sodium	497	mg

---

*To reduce the sodium by 265 mg, substitute onion powder for the onion salt.

COTTAGE CHEESE CANOES

4 celery sticks
½ cup low-fat cottage cheese
Paprika

1. Wash celery sticks and cut into 3- to 4-inch pieces.
2. Fill "canoes" (celery sticks) with cottage cheese.
3. Sprinkle with paprika. Let your child sprinkle; he will like to try.

Yield: 4 servings

Nutrition Information per Serving

Calories	35	
Protein	4	g
Carbohydrate	3	g
Fat	1	g
Cholesterol	2	mg
Sodium	178	mg

☆

CHEESE KABOBS

4 ounces cheddar cheese
4 ounces mozzarella cheese
Assorted fruits, such as grapes, strawberries, bananas, apple wedges

1. Cut cheese into cubes. Wash and prepare fruit into bite-size pieces.
2. Alternate cheese and fruit on a toothpick or skewer. Let your child help create his own!

Yield: 6 servings

Nutrition Information per Serving		
Calories	178	
Protein	9	g
Carbohydrate	13	g
Fat	11	g
Cholesterol	35	mg
Sodium	189	mg

Poultry, Fish, Meat, Nuts, and Beans

The meat group is important because it provides protein as well as iron, zinc, and vitamins B_6 and B_{12}. Lean beef, veal, lamb, pork, fish, chicken, and turkey, as well as eggs, dry beans, dry peas, lentils, and nuts are included in the meat group. (Substituting ground turkey for ground beef in any of the recipes will decrease fat content.) Nutritionists tell us that only two 2- to 3-ounce servings a day are needed by adults or children. We find that if you offer your child a little protein (perhaps 1 ounce of mozzarella "string cheese" or an egg) at breakfast instead of just a sweet cereal or pastry, the breakfast is digested more slowly, and your child is not so ravenous by midmorning.

EGGS IN HATS

4 slices whole wheat bread

4 eggs

4 teaspoons margarine (corn-oil margarine preferred)

1. With a small glass, cookie cutter, or biscuit cutter, cut circles from the center of slices of bread and set aside.
2. Melt 1 teaspoon margarine in skillet.
3. Place bread in pan and break egg into the center of the bread. Cook on both sides until done.
4. Remove when done and place the inside circle of bread on top of the egg to make a "hat".

Yield: 4 servings

Nutrition Information per Serving		
Calories	174	
Protein	8.5	g
Carbohydrate	12	g
Fat	10.5	g
Cholesterol	274	mg
Sodium	272	mg

EGGS IN HATS

BEEF TACOS

This easy-to-make food has all four food groups represented in it! Serve it with milk and let it be the whole supper. Let your child help assemble the tacos.

12 taco shells
1 pound extra-lean ground beef
1 onion, chopped
8-ounce can tomato sauce
Chili powder to taste
Lettuce, chopped
Tomatoes, chopped
1 cup cheddar cheese, grated
Taco sauce, if desired

1. Heat taco shells according to directions on package.
2. Brown ground beef and chopped onion.
3. Drain off all excess fat.
4. Stir in tomato sauce and chili powder.
5. Cook 10-15 minutes on medium heat.
6. Fill shells with meat mixture, tomatoes, lettuce, and cheddar cheese.
7. Drizzle on taco sauce as desired.

Yield: 6 servings (2 tacos per serving)

Nutrition Information per Serving		
Calories	404	
Protein	23	g
Carbohydrate	24	g
Fat	25	g
Cholesterol	103	mg
Sodium	658	mg

QUICK AND EASY CHILI SURPRISE

QUICK AND EASY CHILI SURPRISE

1 pound extra-lean ground beef
1 medium onion, chopped
16-ounce can pinto or kidney beans
10-ounce can tomato soup
2 teaspoons chili powder
Cheddar cheese strips

1. Brown ground beef and onion. Drain off all excess fat.
2. Add remaining ingredients and stir well.
3. Cover and simmer for 30 minutes. Stir occasionally to prevent sticking.
4. For the surprise, place a strip of cheddar cheese (or other favorite cheese) in the bottom of an individual serving bowl. Place the chili on top of the cheese. Just wait to see your child's surprise when he discovers the warm, melted cheese!

Yield: 6 servings

Nutrition Information per Serving		
Calories	380	
Protein	26	g
Carbohydrate	22	g
Fat	21	g
Cholesterol	104	mg
Sodium	719	mg

OVEN-FRIED FISH

1½ pound fish fillets
3 tablespoons cornmeal
3 tablespoons dry bread crumbs
¼ teaspoon paprika
⅛ teaspoon dried dill weed
Dash of pepper
¼ cup skim milk
2 tablespoons corn-oil margarine, melted
Vegetable cooking spray

1. Preheat oven to 450°.
2. Cut fish fillets into 2 × 1½-inch pieces.
3. Mix cornmeal, bread crumbs, paprika, dill weed, and pepper.
4. Dip fish into milk, then coat with cornmeal mixture.
5. Spray pan with cooking spray.
6. Place fish in pan and pour margarine over fish.
7. Cook uncovered until fish flakes easily with fork, about 10-15 minutes.

Yield: 4 servings (6 ounces each)

Nutrition Information per Serving		
Calories	214	
Protein	27	g
Carbohydrate	10	g
Fat	7	g
Cholesterol	0	
Sodium	200	mg

BEEF KABOBS

BEEF KABOBS

Children love to create their own combinations! Let yours pick and choose the vegetables he wants.

2 pounds lean beef (round steak that is cubed)
Assorted vegetables
12 cherry tomatoes
2 onions, cubed
12 mushrooms
2 bell peppers, cubed
Barbecue sauce

1. Alternate vegetables and beef cubes on a skewer.
2. Brush with barbecue sauce.
3. Broil in oven or cook outside on the grill, turning occasionally and brushing with barbecue sauce. Cook for approximately 20 to 30 minutes or until meat and vegetables are tender.

Yield: 6 servings

Nutrition Information per Serving		
Calories	420	
Protein	57	g
Carbohydrate	11	g
Fat	16	g
Cholesterol	161	mg
Sodium	273	mg

FISH STICK FONDUE

2 packages frozen fish sticks (7 ounces each)

Dip #1

1½ cup low-calorie salad dressing (such as Thousand Island)

1 large dill pickle, chopped

½ teaspoon onion powder

Dip #2

½ cup chili sauce

1 teaspoon horseradish

1 teaspoon lemon juice

¼ teaspoon Worcestershire sauce

1. Preheat oven to temperature recommended on fish stick package.
2. Let fish defrost for 10 minutes. Cut each stick into three equal pieces.
3. Place on ungreased cookie sheet.
4. Bake until done according to directions on package.
5. While fish is baking, prepare both dips by combining ingredients and mixing thoroughly.
6. Serve with toothpicks or fondue forks.

Yield: 6 servings

Nutrition Information per Serving		
Calories	240	
Protein	14	g
Carbohydrate	14	g
Fat	14	g
Cholesterol	54	mg
Sodium	794	mg

FISH STICK FONDUE

PIZZA PORK CHOPS

4 pork chops, ¾-inch cut, extra lean
¼ teaspoon oregano
8-ounce can pizza sauce
4 tablespoons onion, chopped
3-ounce can mushrooms, sliced
1 bell pepper, chopped
4-ounce package shredded mozzarella cheese

1. Preheat oven to 350°.
2. Trim all excess fat off of pork chops and place chops in baking dish.
3. Sprinkle pork chops with oregano.
4. Pour pizza sauce over pork chops.
5. Place mushrooms, onions, and bell pepper on top of sauce.
6. Cover with foil. Bake for 1 hour or until pork chops are done.
7. Remove from oven and sprinkle cheese over pork chops. Return to oven until cheese has melted.

Yield: 4 servings

Nutrition Information per Serving		
Calories	447	
Protein	35	g
Carbohydrate	8.6	g
Fat	29	g
Cholesterol	103	mg
Sodium	769	mg

☆

PORCUPINE MEATBALLS

1 egg
10-ounce can condensed tomato soup
¼ cup long-grain rice
1 tablespoon dried parsley flakes
2 tablespoons onion, chopped
Dash pepper
1 pound extra-lean ground beef
¾ cup water
1 teaspoon Worcestershire sauce

1. Mix the egg, ¼ cup tomato soup, rice, parsley flakes, onion, pepper, and ground beef. Blend well.
2. Shape meat mixture into 1-inch meatballs.
3. Place meatballs in skillet and brown on all sides. Drain fat from skillet.
4. Mix remaining soup, water, and Worcestershire sauce.
5. Cook on low heat for approximately 40 minutes or until meatballs are done.

Yield: 4 servings

Nutrition Information per Serving		
Calories	373	
Protein	26	g
Carbohydrate	15	g
Fat	23	g
Cholesterol	195	mg
Sodium	519	mg

PORCUPINE MEATBALLS

FISH STICK TACOS

8 frozen fish sticks
8 taco shells
1 cup chopped lettuce
½ cup chopped tomatoes
1 cup grated cheese

1. Prepare fish sticks according to directions on package.
2. Prepare taco shells according to directions on package.
3. Assemble taco by placing a fish stick in a taco shell first. Then top with lettuce, tomato, and cheese.

Yield:　4 servings (2 tacos per serving)

Nutrition Information per Serving		
Calories	312	
Protein	17	g
Carbohydrate	22	g
Fat	18	g
Cholesterol	61	mg
Sodium	404	mg

FISH STICK TACOS

FRANK KABOBS

8 beef, pork, or turkey frankfurters
12 cherry tomatoes
2 bell peppers
2 onions
1 can baby canned potatoes
Barbecue sauce

1. Cut frankfurters into bite-size pieces.
2. Prepare vegetables by washing and cutting into bite-size pieces.
3. Place on skewer or toothpicks. Alternate frankfurters and vegetables. Let your child help. He will love making his own.
4. Brush with barbecue sauce and broil for approximately 15 minutes.

Yield: 4 servings

Nutrition Information per Serving		
Calories	417	
Protein	15	g
Carbohydrate	29	g
Fat	27	g
Cholesterol	44	mg
Sodium	1,277	mg

OVEN-BAKED CHICKEN DRUMSTICKS

Children enjoy drumsticks because they are easy to handle. You can easily substitute other chicken pieces for the adults in the family.

1 cup cornflake crumbs
¾ teaspoon paprika
½ teaspoon garlic powder
¼ teaspoon ground thyme
¼ teaspoon pepper
6 drumsticks, skinned
½ cup low-fat buttermilk
Vegetable cooking spray

1. Combine cornflake crumbs, paprika, garlic powder, thyme, and pepper in a plastic bag. Mix well.
2. Dip chicken in buttermilk, coating well. Then shake in bag to coat with cornflake crumbs.
3. Spray baking dish with cooking spray. Place chicken in pan.
4. Bake, uncovered, at 400° for 45 minutes or until done.

Yield: 6 servings

Nutrition Information per Serving		
Calories	105	
Protein	14	g
Carbohydrate	5.5	g
Fat	3	g
Cholesterol	42	mg
Sodium	115	mg

BIG-EYE "PIZZAS"

1 pound extra-lean ground beef
½ cup dry bread crumbs
8-ounce can tomato sauce
½ teaspoon oregano
½ cup shredded mozzarella cheese
½ cup shredded cheddar cheese
4 pimento-stuffed olives
4 slices canned pimento

1. Preheat oven to 425°.
2. Mix ground beef, bread crumbs, ½ cup tomato sauce, and oregano.
3. Divide ground beef mixture into four parts. Form into 4-inch circles. Pinch edge of each circle to form a rim. Place in low baking dish.
4. Pour 2 tablespoons of tomato sauce onto each circle. Spread it out evenly.
5. Bake 20 minutes.
6. Remove from oven. Sprinkle mozzarella cheese on bottom half for face and cheddar cheese on top half for hair.
7. Cut olives in half. Add the olives for the eyes and the pimento strips for the smile.
8. Return pizzas to the oven. Bake another 5 minutes or until cheese has melted.

Yield: 4 servings

Nutrition Information per Serving		
Calories	494	
Protein	35.5	g
Carbohydrate	17	g
Fat	31	g
Cholesterol	158	mg
Sodium	1,039	mg

EGGS IN BOLOGNA CUPS

Nonstick spray
6 slices of turkey bologna
6 eggs
6 teaspoons milk
Salt (optional)
Pepper
Paprika

1. Preheat oven to 375°.
2. Spray muffin tin with nonstick spray.
3. Heat bologna pieces until warm and centers begin to puff.
4. Place each in muffin tin and press down so it fits inside cup.
5. Break one egg into center of each cup.
6. Pour 1 teaspoon milk over each egg.
7. Season to taste.
8. Bake uncovered 15-20 minutes or until egg is done.

Yield: 6 servings

Nutrition Information per Serving		
Calories	144	
Protein	10	g
Carbohydrate	1.8	g
Fat	10	g
Cholesterol	295	mg
Sodium	294	mg*

---

*Nutrition information does not include your addition of salt. Please note that added salt really isn't needed because of the salt in the bologna.

☆

BROILED SALMON BUNS

2 cans salmon, 7¾ ounces each
6 boiled eggs, chopped
⅓ cup pickle relish
⅔ cup low-calorie mayonnaise
6 hamburger buns, split

1. Drain and flake salmon.
2. Add eggs, pickle relish and mayonnaise.
3. Spread salmon mixture on hamburger buns.
4. Broil in oven until brown, approximately 5 minutes.

Yield:　6 servings

Nutrition Information per Serving		
Calories	440	
Protein	26	g
Carbohydrate	27	g
Fat	26	g
Cholesterol	309	mg
Sodium	821	mg

BROILED SALMON BUNS

TASTY TUNA CHEESEBURGER

6½-ounce can water-packed tuna, drained
¼ cup chopped celery
¼ cup chopped green pepper
¼ to ½ cup low-calorie buttermilk salad dressing
½ cup diced cheddar cheese
4 sandwich buns, preferably whole wheat

1. Flake tuna with a fork.
2. Add celery and green pepper.
3. Add enough dressing to moisten.
4. Add cheese. Mix well.
5. Spoon onto sandwich buns. Wrap in aluminum foil.
6. Heat at 350° for 20 minutes. Serve hot.

Yield: 4 servings

Nutrition Information per Serving		
Calories	264	
Protein	19	g
Carbohydrate	22	g
Fat	11	g
Cholesterol	42	mg
Sodium	689	mg

TASTY TUNA CHEESEBURGER

CHICKEN BUNDLES

4 boneless chicken breasts
4 slices Swiss or mozzarella cheese, 1 ounce each
4 broccoli spears
Pimento strips
12-ounce can cream of mushroom soup
½ cup low-fat milk
2 green onions, chopped

1. Preheat oven to 375°.
2. Pound chicken breasts to flatten.
3. Place 1 slice of cheese over each chicken breast.
4. Place 1 broccoli spear in center of each chicken breast.
5. Roll chicken breast securing with a toothpick. Place pimento strips on top, as if they were tying the bundles together.
6. Place seam-side down in rectangular baking dish.
7. Combine mushroom soup and milk. Pour over chicken breasts.
8. Sprinkle onions on top.
9. Bake at above temperature for 50 minutes.

Yield: 4 servings

Nutrition Information per Serving		
Calories	410	
Protein	43	g
Carbohydrate	16	g
Fat	19.5	g
Cholesterol	102	mg
Sodium	848	mg

CRATER HAM LOAF

1 pound ground cooked smoked ham
1 pound ground lean pork
2 eggs
3 cups whole wheat flake cereal
1 cup low-fat milk
⅛ teaspoon pepper

CHEESE TOPPING

1 egg
2 tablespoons low-fat milk
4 ounces shredded cheddar or other favorite cheese
¼ teaspoon dry mustard
¼ teaspoon Worcestershire sauce

1. Preheat oven to 375°.
2. Mix thoroughly the ground ham, ground pork, eggs, whole wheat cereal, low-fat milk, and pepper.
3. Shape into round mound. Depress in center to form a crater.
4. Prepare cheese topping. Mix 1 egg and 2 tablespoons milk. Stir in cheese, dry mustard, and Worcestershire sauce.
5. Pour cheese topping over meat mixture.
6. Bake for 1 hour.

Yield: 8 servings

Nutrition Information per Serving		
Calories	435	
Protein	37	g
Carbohydrate	11	g
Fat	24	g
Cholesterol	217	mg
Sodium	1,090	mg*

*Please note that we left extra salt out of the recipe. It's not needed because of the salt that's in the ham.

☆

SPAGHETTI SAUCE

This is a new way to lower the fat content of ground beef dishes. Use half extra-lean ground beef and half ground turkey.

- ¾ **pound extra-lean ground beef**
- ¾ **pound ground turkey**
- **1½ cups chopped onions**
- **1 cup chopped green pepper**
- **1½ cups chopped celery**
- **28-ounce can Italian plum tomatoes**
- **6-ounce can tomato paste**
- **1 teaspoon black pepper**
- **1 teaspoon oregano**
- **½ teaspoon basil**
- **½ teaspoon garlic powder**
- **2 teaspoons Worcestershire sauce**
- **2-3 bay leaves**

1. Mix ground meats and brown in a large pot. Cook until brown. Drain off all extra fat.
2. Add onions, pepper, and celery. Cook until slightly tender.
3. Add remaining ingredients. Cover. Simmer for 2 hours.
4. A trick to remove fat: Before serving, let the sauce cool. Place in refrigerator. Skim off the fat that hardens on the surface before reheating.
5. Serve sauce over pasta and sprinkle with parmesan cheese if desired.

Yield: 8 servings

Nutrition Information per Serving		
Calories	269	
Protein	22	g
Carbohydrate	15	g
Fat	14	g
Cholesterol	86	mg
Sodium	275	mg

Healthy Snack Foods

Kids and snacks—they're a perfect combination. At a time when children are growing, snacks can give them a nutrition boost. Snacks should be quick, easy, and good-tasting, as well as nutritious.

If you or your child is hungry, you often grab the first thing in sight. The trick is to have only the right things in sight. Stock up on fresh fruits, real fruit juices, yogurt, cheese, nuts, whole grain or enriched crackers, or any other foods from the four main food groups. Most commercial prepackaged snacks are high in calories, fat, and sugar. Take a little time to prepare your own healthy snacks.

Use snacks that supplement your child's diet with valuable nutrients. Then snacking isn't bad for him. Remember to keep your eye on your main goal—a balanced diet. Use snack time as a time to enhance the food group that might have been neglected that day.

Low-calorie snacks are generally

- bulky, like unbuttered popcorn;
- thin and watery, like juices; or
- crisp but not greasy, like most vegetables and many fruits.

Food is generally higher in calories if it is

- oily or greasy, like French fries;
- smooth, slick, or gooey, like hot fudge sauce; or
- sweet, sticky, and compact, like pastries.

To further help you choose healthy snacks, here are a few suggestions:

- All fresh fruits are good choices. Fruits canned in water or light syrup are also acceptable. Avoid sweetened fruits.
- All fresh, frozen, or canned vegetables make good choices. Try them with dips. Your child will love them.
- Many breads are good choices: bagels; English muffins; French or Italian bread; pita bread; and rye, sourdough, whole wheat, and multigrain breads. Serve them with fruit butters, low-fat dips, or reduced-calorie cheeses.
- Choose low-fat dairy products: skim and low-fat milk, buttermilk, low-fat cheeses, low-fat yogurt, ices, sherbet, and ice milk.
- Baked goods can be good choices if made at home using low-fat, low-sugar ingredients.

- Air-popped popcorn is an excellent snack; season with pepper, herbs, or a little parmesan cheese.
- Water remains the best beverage to serve your child. Serve with a little lemon juice. Fruit juices and homemade low-fat milkshakes are also good choices. On a cold day, cocoa made with low-fat milk and cocoa powder can be a treat as well as nourishing.

GRILLED PEANUT BUTTER AND BANANA SANDWICH

1 slice bread, preferably whole wheat
2 tablespoons peanut butter
½ small banana, mashed

1. Spread peanut butter on open-face bread.
2. Spread mashed banana over peanut butter layer.
3. Broil until hot and brown on top.

Yield: 1 serving

Nutrition Information per Serving		
Calories	300	
Protein	12	g
Carbohydrate	30	g
Fat	17	g
Cholesterol	0	
Sodium	317	mg

GRILLED PEANUT BUTTER AND BANANA SANDWICH

FROZEN FRUITS

FROZEN FRUITS

Freeze a variety of fresh fruits. Try grapes and bite-sized pieces of pineapple, peaches, pears, cantaloupe, watermelon, bananas, and so on. Let your child choose his favorites. Stick each with a toothpick and watch these coolers disappear. These snacks are low in calories and sugar—great as a summertime cooler.

Nutrition Information per Serving (1 cup)					
	Pineapple Chunks	Banana	Canteloupe	Peaches	Watermelon
Calories	77	105	57	74	50
Protein	.6 g	1.2 g	1.4 g	1.2 g	1 g
Carbohydrate	19.2 g	26.7 g	13.4 g	19.4 g	11.5 g
Fat	.7 g	.6 g	.4 g	trace	.7 g
Cholesterol	0	0	0	0	0
Sodium	1 mg	1 mg	14 mg	0	3 mg

RAISIN BREAD SUPREME

RAISIN BREAD SUPREME

This is a quick and easy snack!

1 slice raisin bread
2 tablespoons peanut butter

1. Toast raisin bread.
2. Spread with peanut butter.

Yield: 1 serving

Nutrition Information per Serving		
Calories	242	
Protein	10	g
Carbohydrate	20	g
Fat	15	g
Cholesterol	0	
Sodium	251	mg

FRUIT GELATIN BLOCKS

1½ cup water
3 envelopes unflavored gelatin
6-ounce can frozen juice concentrate: orange, apple,
grape, or cranberry

1. Pour water into a medium saucepan.
2. Sprinkle gelatin over water.
3. Let stand 1 minute and bring to a boil, stirring constantly until gelatin dissolves.
4. Remove from heat. Let cool.
5. Stir in frozen juice concentrate. Stir until mixed well.
6. Pour into foil-lined 8-by-8-by-2-inch pan.
7. Cover and chill until firm.
8. Invert pan and empty onto waxed paper.
9. Cut into squares.

Yield: 36 servings

Nutrition Information per Serving		
Calories	13	
Protein	0.5	g
Carbohydrate	3	g
Fat	trace	
Cholesterol	0	
Sodium	1	mg

FRUIT GELATIN BLOCKS

APPLE-PEANUT-RAISIN GOODIES

1 medium apple
4 tablespoons peanut butter
2 tablespoons raisins

1. Core and cut apple into 8 wedges.
2. Spread peanut butter on wedges.
3. Divide raisins between wedges and place on top of peanut butter.
4. Serve immediately. Otherwise, to keep apple pieces from turning brown, you can dip them in lemon juice prior to adding peanut butter and raisins.

Yield: 2 servings

Nutrition Information per Serving

Calories	255	
Protein	9	g
Carbohydrate	23	g
Fat	16	g
Cholesterol	0	
Sodium	159	mg

☆

FROZEN BANANA ROCKETS

1 medium banana
1 tablespoon honey
2 tablespoons chopped walnuts

1. Cut banana in half.
2. Coat banana half with honey.
3. Roll banana in walnuts.
4. Freeze until firm.

Yield: 2 servings

Nutrition Information per Serving		
Calories	132	
Protein	2	g
Carbohydrate	23	g
Fat	5	g
Cholesterol	0	
Sodium	1	mg

FROZEN FRUIT JUICE POPS

Pour your child's favorite unsweetened fruit juice into paper cups. Let them partially freeze. Add wooden sticks in centers. Return to freezer until firm. Peel paper from pops and serve.

Nutrition Information per Serving (1 ounce cup per serving)				
	Orange Juice	Grape Juice	Apple Juice	Cranberry Juice	Pineapple Juice
Calories	52	78	58	74	70
Protein	trace	.7 g	trace	trace	.4 g
Carbohydrate	12 g	19 g	15 g	19 g	17 g
Fat	trace	trace	trace	trace	trace
Cholesterol	0	0	0	0	0
Sodium	1 mg	3.5 mg	3.5 mg	5 mg	.1 mg

CHEWY CRUNCHERS

1 cup Grape Nuts cereal
½ cup raisins
½ cup sunflower seeds

Mix ingredients.

Yield: 2 cups

Nutrition Information per Serving (¼ cup)		
Calories	157	
Protein	5	g
Carbohydrate	22	g
Fat	7	g
Cholesterol	0	
Sodium	104	mg

BANANA BOATS (CANOES)

1 medium banana, peeled
2 tablespoons peanut butter

1. Cut a medium-sized wedge down the length of the banana.
2. Fill with peanut butter.
3. Call it a canoe and mound the peanut butter up, like Indians sitting in a canoe.

Yield: 1 serving

Nutrition Information per Serving		
Calories	291	
Protein	10	g
Carbohydrate	32	g
Fat	16	g
Cholesterol	0	
Sodium	158	mg

PUMPKIN SEEDS

Kids love to help take the seeds out of the pumpkin!

Pumpkin seeds (as many as the pumpkin had in it)
2 tablespoons safflower or corn oil, if desired
Salt, if desired

1. Preheat oven to 325°.
2. Mix pumpkin seeds with oil if you plan to salt them.
3. Spread seeds out on baking sheet.
4. Bake 8-10 minutes until brown.
5. Sprinkle with salt, if desired.*

Yield: Varies according to size of pumpkin

Nutrition Information per Serving (1 ounce)		
Calories	155	
Protein	8	g
Carbohydrate	4	g
Fat	13	g
Cholesterol	0	
Sodium	140	mg

---

*If you omit the salt, sodium content is a trace.

GRILLED PEANUT BUTTER-AND-JELLY SANDWICH

GRILLED PEANUT BUTTER-AND-JELLY SANDWICH

2 slices whole wheat bread
2 tablespoons peanut butter
1 tablespoon jelly*
Corn-oil margarine

1. Spread 1 slice of bread with peanut butter and the other with jelly. Close sandwich.
2. Spread softened margarine on outside of both slices of bread.
3. Grill until brown on both sides.

Yield: 1 serving

Nutrition Information per Serving		
Calories	397	
Protein	14	g
Carbohydrate	43	g
Fat	22	g
Cholesterol	0	
Sodium	522	mg

*Try the low-sugar and -calorie jellies such as Smuckers or Polaner and call it "No Belly Jelly".

MINIPIZZAS

1 English muffin, split
4 tablespoons tomato sauce
¼ teaspoon oregano
4 tablespoons mozzarella cheese

1. Place English muffins on cookie sheet.
2. Top each half with tomato sauce, oregano, and mozzarella cheese.
3. Broil in oven until cheese melts.

Yield: 2 servings

Nutrition Information per Serving		
Calories	243	
Protein	15	g
Carbohydrate	16	g
Fat	13	g
Cholesterol	44	mg
Sodium	573	mg

CHEERIOS NECKLACE

Cheerios
Large darning needle
Brightly colored yarn

When your child is looking for something to do, provide him with the above items. Tie a Cheerio to one end of a length of yarn; then your child threads more Cheerios onto the yarn. Make a necklace by tying the ends of the yarn together. Let your child wear this edible necklace (the yarn is inedible though!).

Nutrition Information per Serving (½ cup)	
Calories	44
Protein	1.7 g
Carbohydrate	8 g
Fat	0.7 g
Cholesterol	0
Sodium	123 mg

HOMEMADE PEANUT BUTTER

No salt or sugar added! Your child will love to watch the peanuts turn to peanut butter.

2 cups unsalted roasted peanuts

1. Place peanuts in blender container.
2. Cover and blend at low speed until finely chopped, about 1-2 minutes.
3. Blend at high speed, stopping blender occasionally to scrape sides. Blend to smooth consistency, approximately 7-8 minutes.
4. Cover and refrigerate.

Yield: 1 cup

Nutrition Information per Serving (1 tablespoon)		
Calories	85	
Protein	4.3	g
Carbohydrate	3	g
Fat	7	g
Cholesterol	0	
Sodium	1	mg

NACHO POPCORN

¼ cup corn-oil margarine
1 teaspoon paprika
¼ teaspoon red pepper
½ teaspoon ground cumin
10 cups warm popped popcorn
½ cup parmesan cheese

1. Melt margarine in a small saucepan and stir in paprika, pepper, and cumin.
2. Drizzle mixture over warm popcorn and gently toss.
3. Sprinkle with parmesan cheese and toss until mixed well.

Yield: 5 servings (2 cups each)

Nutrition Information per Serving		
Calories	245	
Protein	6	g
Carbohydrate	22	g
Fat	12	g
Cholesterol	5	mg
Sodium	218	mg

APPLESAUCE TOAST

1 tablespoon corn-oil margarine
2 tablespoons sugar
1 cup applesauce
Cinnamon and nutmeg to taste
4 slices whole wheat bread

1. Melt margarine and combine with sugar, applesauce, cinnamon, and nutmeg.
2. Spread mixture on bread. Broil bread in oven until brown.
3. Serve hot.

Yield: 4 servings

Nutrition Information per Serving		
Calories	136	
Protein	2.5	g
Carbohydrate	25	g
Fat	4	g
Cholesterol	0	
Sodium	193	mg

APPLESAUCE TOAST

SLEEPING PICKLE

2 slices whole wheat bread
2 slices extra-lean ham
1 whole dill or sweet pickle, cut in half lengthwise
2 slices cheese (your child's favorite kind)

1. Place bread on cookie sheet.
2. Place ham on top of bread.
3. Place pickle on top of the ham.
4. Top each with a cheese slice, covering all but one end of the pickle. Let the pickle "nap" in the oven until the cheese melts and the bread is toasted.
5. Bake at 400° for 6 to 7 minutes.

Yield: 2 servings

Nutrition Information per Serving		
Calories	224	
Protein	18	g
Carbohydrate	13	g
Fat	13	g
Cholesterol	71	mg
Sodium	1,574	mg

Foods for Kids on the Go

Whether you are packing a lunch for school or a picnic, you can pack food from the same four basic food groups as you would if you were eating at home.

When packing a lunch, pack it a little fancier because you're not there to serve it. If it's for an older child (who can read), slip in a little "love note" for him. Offer warm and cold foods. A thermos can keep a soup or stew hot or keep juice or fruit cold. Instead of chips, include raw vegetables for your child to munch on. Be creative and add variety!

When traveling, before you leave decide whether you are going to bring food along. If not, think of what kind of restaurant you will eat in. When eating out, don't be afraid to ask for your food to be prepared without added salt, sugar, or fat. Have an idea in mind of what you would like to eat before you arrive at the restaurant; discuss it with your child. Order, then pass a low-calorie snack to him while you wait.

When traveling, you may also want to carry along some nutritious snacks for your child to munch on. This will ensure that he gets healthy snacks and will also eliminate making unnecessary stops along the way. Carry along a wash cloth in a plastic bag for easy cleanups! Most of all, relax and enjoy yourself and your child.

POPCORN BALLS

6 cups popped popcorn
¼ cup honey
⅓ cup peanut butter

1. Put popcorn in a large pan.
2. Place in a 250° oven to keep warm.
3. Heat honey to boiling point in a small saucepan.
4. Add peanut butter and stir until well blended.
5. Remove warm popcorn and drizzle with hot mixture.
6. Stir popcorn to coat evenly.
7. Tear off 10 sheets of wax paper, each approximately 12 by 12 inches.
8. Divide popcorn evenly among 10 sheets of waxed paper.
9. Fold corners of paper up around popcorn and twist top. Press popcorn to make balls.
10. Store in airtight container.

Yield: 10 servings

Nutrition Information per Serving		
Calories	106	
Protein	4	g
Carbohydrate	14	g
Fat	5	g
Cholesterol	0	
Sodium	42	mg

POPCORN BALLS

BANANA CHIPS

4 medium bananas
¼ cup lemon juice

1. Slice bananas and dip into lemon juice.
2. Place on an oiled baking sheet in a single layer.
3. Bake at 175° for 2-3 hours, until golden brown.
4. Store in airtight container.

Yield: 4 servings

Nutrition Information per Serving		
Calories	109	
Protein	1.3	g
Carbohydrate	28	g
Fat	0.6	g
Cholesterol	0	
Sodium	1	mg

SESAME CRUNCH CANDY

½ cup creamy peanut butter
½ cup honey
2 cups cornflakes
1 cup sesame seeds

1. Mix first 3 ingredients.
2. Chill in refrigerator for 15 minutes.
3. Form into balls using 1 tablespoon mixture per ball.
4. Roll in sesame seeds.

Yield: 50 servings

Nutrition Information per Serving		
Calories	56	
Protein	2	g
Carbohydrate	5	g
Fat	4	g
Cholesterol	0	
Sodium	26	mg

BANANA CHIPS

SESAME CRUNCH CANDY

PINEAPPLE COOKIES

1 cup crushed pineapple
1⅓ cups nonfat dry powdered milk
½ teaspoon vanilla
2 teaspoons sugar

1. Mix all ingredients.
2. Drop by spoonfuls onto greased cookie sheet.
3. Bake at 350° for 15-20 minutes or until edges are golden brown.

Yield: 12 cookies

Nutrition Information per Serving		
Calories	42	
Protein	3	g
Carbohydrate	7	g
Fat	trace	
Cholesterol	1.5	mg
Sodium	42	mg

MOZZARELLA STRING CHEESE

A quick delight for lunch boxes or snacking. Give a younger child half of a log of cheese. Show him how to pull off a "string" of cheese; watch him eat and enjoy.

Nutrition Information per Serving (2 ounce)		
Calories	180	
Protein	12.2	g
Carbohydrate	1.4	g
Fat	14	g
Cholesterol	50	mg
Sodium	236	mg

DRIED FRUIT ROLL-UPS

Take a little time to make your own fruit roll-ups. They're lower in sugar than commercial ones and don't contain preservatives.

10 ounces dried fruit, such as dried apples, pears, peaches, apricots, or a mixture.
1¾ cups water
Nonstick vegetable spray

1. Combine dried fruit and water in a medium saucepan.
2. Bring to a boil, then reduce heat.
3. Simmer until fruit is very tender.
4. Drain off any excess liquid, if necessary.
5. Cool.
6. Blend fruit in blender until smooth.
7. Line a baking pan with foil and spray with the nonstick spray.
8. Spread fruit in a thin layer over foil.
9. Bake at 300° for 25 minutes.
10. Without opening door, turn off oven and let dry 8 hours or overnight.
11. Lift foil out of baking pan and remove fruit from foil.
12. Roll up fruit and store in airtight container.
13. Let kids tear off pieces as desired.

Yield: 12-inch roll, 4 servings

Nutrition Information per Serving		
Calories	173	
Protein	2	g
Carbohydrate	46	g
Fat	0.3	g
Cholesterol	0	
Sodium	13	mg

☆

NIBBLES

**5 cups mixed dry cereal, such as Cheerios, Wheat or
Rice Chex, Shredded Wheat, or Puffed Corn or
Rice cereals**

2 cups pretzels, broken in pieces

⅓ cup corn-oil margarine

4 teaspoons Worcestershire sauce

1 teaspoon celery flakes

½ teaspoon onion powder

½ teaspoon garlic powder

1 cup mixed nuts

1. Combine dry cereals and pretzels.
2. Melt margarine in a saucepan and combine with Worcestershire sauce and seasonings.
3. Toss margarine mixture with cereals.
4. Add mixed nuts.
5. Place in a shallow roasting pan. Bake at 275° for 1 hour, stirring every 10-15 minutes.

Yield: 8 cups

Nutrition Information per Serving		
Calories	282	
Protein	4.6	g
Carbohydrate	24	g
Fat	19	g
Cholesterol	0	
Sodium	399	mg

APPLE SNACK

APPLE SNACK

2 quarts apples

1. Peel, core, and halve apples.
2. Shred apples coarsely and put on a cookie sheet that has been coated with nonstick vegetable spray.
3. Bake at 250° until apples are dry.
4. Let cool.
5. Store in airtight container.

Yield: 8 servings

Nutrition Information per Serving		
Calories	162	
Protein	0.6	g
Carbohydrate	42	g
Fat	1	g
Cholesterol	0	
Sodium	2	mg

PEANUT BUTTER-AND-JELLY SANDWICH

The all-time favorite of kids and adults. Make it with raisin bread or add a banana! Whatever the combination, it is sure to be a winner.

2 slices whole wheat bread
2 tablespoons peanut butter
2 tablespoons grape jelly*

1. Spread peanut butter and jelly on bread.
2. Close sandwich.

Yield: 1 serving

Nutrition Information per Serving		
Calories	404	
Protein	13	g
Carbohydrate	57	g
Fat	17	g
Cholesterol	0	
Sodium	586	mg

---

*Use low-sugar and low-calorie brands.

LUNCH BOX TREATS

This is great to include in your child's lunch box for school!

2 cups sunflower seeds, unsalted
½ cup walnuts
1 cup soynuts
1 cup peanuts
1 cup raisins

1. Combine all ingredients. Mix well.
2. Store in airtight container.

Yield: 10½ cups

Nutrition Information per Serving
(½ cup)

Calories	236	
Protein	11	g
Carbohydrate	13	g
Fat	17	g
Cholesterol	0	
Sodium	8	mg

LUNCH BOX TREATS

Epilogue

If you follow the plan of the previous chapters, you will be getting your child off to an early start on a well way of life. Parents and others involved in early childhood education can encourage physical fitness and nutrition principles and practices that will foster the healthy and happy adults of the 21st Century. In reading this book, you have been furthering a design that will prevent obesity and other eating disorders as well as sedentary living. You have been building the total health and well-being of the whole child.

A major purpose for writing this book is to help all preschool educators (parents, teachers, relatives, neighbors, etc.) become more aware of the importance and impact of their interactions with children. It is not just what you do at these various stages, but also how you do it that can lead to the creation of the truly healthy child. It need not be your purpose to develop a Superbaby, or to create numerous geniuses (Pressey, 1964). Rather, your goal is to help each child, with his or her unique genetic blueprint, develop to his fullest capability in an atmosphere of love. Your ability to influence growth and development recognizes the impact that the environment has on the total child's growth:

- Physically, with more optimal and preventive health
- Mentally, with maximum intellectual growth due to positive interactions with the environment
- Emotionally, with fuller realization of your love and caring as you spend your time, energy, talents, and involvement interacting with your child

Progress does not occur in isolation, but development is enhanced when mind, body, and spirit work in unison! You need to be more aware of the relationship between the physical and nutritional activity (linked with loving, verbal exchanges) and your child's intellectual and affective development. Thus, you foster the *whole child*.

Lifelong habits and lifestyles are instilled at an early age. The present physical fitness and nutrition movement cannot be complete without including the very young. Indeed, if fitness were started early, many problems would be alleviated or avoided. Interest in exercise, nutrition, and weight control would not be the mania of fat or otherwise unfit American adults. The public would not be spending millions of dollars annually for reducing pills, diet books, exercise equipment, exercise programs, exercise clothing, exercise spas, and gimmicks. Prevention of problems is the key. Obesity and lack of fitness are lifelong problems of adults that are difficult to reverse after years of habituation to sedentary living and poor eating habits. The solution to physical inactivity and obesity lies with the beginning to develop healthy lifestyles in infancy.

We have presented a philosophy of child-rearing that will foster physical fitness and normal body weight through interesting and challenging physical activities and a sensible, sound diet. We integrate this philosophy with practical, pleasurable ideas that can be experienced with your child in a loving environment. Thus, we will challenge and support this future adult. Without such efforts, intellectual, emotional, and physical abilities will be wasted and untold potential will not come to full realization. Such efforts will help determine who your child is and what she will become. These alternatives will help her achieve a happy and healthy childhood today and adulthood in the years 2000, 2001, 2002, and on and on.

References

Americans eating their way to an early grave. (1988, July 27). *The Times* [Gainesville, GA], pp. 5-6.

Behrman, R., & Vaughn, V. (Eds.) (1983). *Nelson textbook of pediatrics* (12th ed.). Philadelphia: W.B. Saunders.

Blessing, P. (1986, September-October). Childhood obesity. *Children Today*, pp. 25-29.

Bloom, B. (1964). *Stability and change in human characteristics*. New York: Wiley.

Boyer, J. (1984). *Feelin' good youth fitness report summary*. Spring Arbor, MI: Fitness Finders.

Brazelton, T.B. (1983). *Infants and mothers: Differences in development*. New York: Delacorte.

Brierley, J. (1976). *The growing brain*. Windsor, Great Britain: NFER.

Caplan, F. (Ed.) (1977). *The parenting advisor*. Garden City, NY: Anchor Press/Doubleday.

Centers for Disease Control. (1987). *Morbidity and Mortality Weekly Report*, **36**(26), 426-430.

Clark, B. (1983). *Growing up gifted*. Columbus OH: Charles E. Merrill.

Committee on Nutrition. (1981). Nutritional Aspects of Obesity in Infancy and Childhood. *Pediatrics*, **68**(6), 880-881.

Davis, A. (1972). *Let's have healthy children*. New York: Harcourt, Brace, & Jovanovich.

Eden, A. (1978, February). Trim talk. *Slim Living Instructor's Newsletter*, p. 136.

Hunt, J., & Kirk, G. (1971). Social aspects of intelligence: Evidence and issues. In R. Cancro (Ed.), *Intelligence: Genetic and environmental influences*. New York: Grune & Stratton.

Iverson, D., Fielding, J., Crow, R., & Christenson, G. (1985). The promotion of physical activity in the United States population: The status of programs in medical, worksite, community, and school settings. *Public Health Report*, **100**, 212-224.

Keats, E. (1962). *The snowy day*. New York: Viking.

Mayer, J. (1976, June 21). Healthy children. *Time*, p. 111.

Morganfield, R. (1988, July 29-31). As classes shrink, kids do better. *USA Today*, p. 42.

Moss, H.A., & Kagan, J. (1958). Maternal influences on early IQ scores. *Psychology Reports, 4*, 661-665.

Picciano, M.F. (1987, January-February). Nutrient needs of infants. *Nutrition Today*, pp. 29-30.

Pipes, P.L. (1984). Nutrition in infancy. In M. Krause & L.K. Mahan (Eds.), *Food, nutrition, and diet therapy*. Philadelphia: W.B. Saunders.

Pisacano, J.C., et al. (1978). An attempt at prevention of obesity in infancy. *Pediatrics, 61*(3), 360-364.

Pooling Project Research Group. (1978). Relationship of blood pressure, serum cholesterol, smoking, relative weight, and ECG abnormalities to incidence of major coronary events: Final report of the Pooling Project. *Journal of Chronic Diseases, 31*, 202-306.

Pressey, S. (1964). The nature and nurture of genius. In J. French (Ed.), *Educating the gifted child*. New York: Holt, Rinehart, and Winston.

Public Health Service. (1980). *Promoting health/preventing disease: Objectives for the nation*. Washington, DC: United States Department of Health and Human Services.

Pugliese, M.T., & Lifshitz, F. (1987). Parental health beliefs as a cause of nonorganic "fail to thrive." *Pediatrics, 80*(2), 880-882.

Rosenzweig, M. (1966). Environmental complexity, cerebral change, and behavior. *American Psychologist, 21*, 321-332.

Safran, C. (1987, August). You are what you think. *Reader's Digest*, pp. 44-49.

Sallis, J., Haskell, W., Fortmann, S., Wood, P., & Vranizan, K. (1985). Moderate-intensity physical activity and cardiovascular risk factors: The Stanford Five-City Project. *Preventive Medicine, 15*, 561-568.

Siscovick, D., LaPorte, R., & Newman, J. (1985). The disease-specific benefits and risks of physical activity and exercise. *Public Health Report, 100*, 195-202.

Skeels, H., & Dye, H. (1959). A study of the effects of differential stimulation on mentally retarded children. *Proceedings of the American Association on Mental Deficiency, 44*, 114-136.

Spock, B. (1971). *Baby and child care*. New York: Pocket Books.

Stephens, P., Hoffman, W., Karlson, K., Campbell, R., & Strong, W. (1988, February). Exercise for children with chronic disease. *Journal of Musculoskeletal Medicine*.

Sutton-Smith, B. (1973). *Child psychology.* New York: Meredith.

Sweeny, C., Smith, H., Foster, J., Place, J., Specht, J., Kochenour, N., & Prater, B. (1985). Effects of nutrition intervention program during pregnancy. *Journal of Nurse-Midwifery,* **30**(3), 61.

Taylor, T., Sallis, J., & Needle, R. (1985). The relationship of physical activity and exercise to mental health. *Public Health Report,* **100**, 195-202.

Teylor, T. (1977). An introduction to the neurosciences. In M. Wittrock (Ed.), *The human brain.* Englewood Cliffs, NJ: Prentice-Hall.

Whaley, L.L., & Wong, D. (1979). *Nursing care of infants and children.* St. Louis: Mosby.

White, B.L. (1987). *Educating the infant and toddler.* Lexington, MA: Lexington Books.

Williams, S.R. (1985). *Essentials of nutrition and diet therapy* (4th ed.). St. Louis: Mosby.

Winn, M. (1985). *The plug-in drug.* New York: Viking.

Suggested Readings

Birch, H., & Gussow, J. (1970). *Disadvantaged children.* New York: Harcourt, Brace, and World.

Caspersen, C., Christenson, G., & Pollard, R. (1985). Status of the 1990 physical fitness and exercise objectives: Evidence form NHIS 1985. *Public Health Report,* **101**, 587-592.

Diagram Group. (1977). *Child's body: A parent's manual.* New York: Paddington Press.

Ferguson, M. (1973). *The brain revolution.* New York: Taplinger.

Harvard Preschool Project. (1979). *The origins of human competence: The final report of the Harvard Preschool Project.* Lexington, MA: Lexington Books.

Hunt, J.M. (1961). *Intelligence and experience.* New York: Ronald Press.

Krech, D. (1969). Psychoneurobiochemeducation. *Phi Delta Kappan,* **50**, 370-375.

Lucan, B. (1984). Nutrition in childhood. In M. Krause & L.K. Mahan (Eds.), *Food, nutrition, and diet therapy.* Philadelphia: W.B. Saunders.

McCandless, B. (1964). Relationship of environmental factors to intellectual functioning. In H. Stevens & R. Heber (Eds.), *Mental retardation.* Chicago: University of Chicago Press.

National Research Council. (1980). *Recommended daily dietary allowances* (Report No. 1694). Washington, DC: Food and Nutrition Board, National Academy of Sciences.

Pennington, J., & Church, H.N. (Eds.) (1985). *Bowes & Church's food values of portions commonly used.* Philadelphia: J.B. Lippincott.

Powell, K., Thompson, P., Casperson, C., & Kendrick, J. (1987). Physical activity and the incidence of coronary heart disease. *Annual Review of Public Health,* **8**, 253-287.

Rooth, G. (1976). *Socio-economic aspects of perinatal medicine.* Symposium presented at the meeting of the Congress of Perinatal Medicine, Uppsala, Sweden.

Sagan, C. (1977). *The dragons of Eden.* New York: Random House.

Smallman, S. (1987, February 4). Nutritional assessment of children in hospital. *Nursing Times*.

Tarjan, G. (1970). Some thoughts on sociocultural retardation. In H.C. Haywood (Ed.), *Socio-cultural aspects of mental retardation*. New York: Appleton-Century-Crofts.

Taylor, C., Sallis, J., & Needle, R. (1985). The relationship of physical activity and exercise to mental health. *Public Health Report*, **100**, 195-202.

Udall, J.A. (1978). Relation between maternal prepregnant weight, weight gain during pregnancy and obesity in infants. *Pediatrics*, **62**, 493.

United States Department of Agriculture. (1975). *Nutritive value of American foods in common units*. Washington, DC: Author.

Wittrock, M. (1980). *The brain and psychology*. New York: Academic Press.

Wishon, P.M., & Kinnick, V.G. (1986). Helping infants overcome the problem of obesity. *American Journal of Maternal/Child Nursing*, **11**, 118-121.

Index

Numbers in italics indicate that entry is an exercise or movement exploration activity.

About the Authors

Helen T. Fish has a master's degree in early childhood education from Brenau College, Gainesville, Georgia, where she is now an adjunct assistant professor in the education department. She has also been a former early childhood and prereading consultant for the University of Wisconsin Research and Development Center. As a participant in the Teacher in Space Program in 1985, Helen won a NASA acknowledgment for her contribution to furthering the role of education in the United States.

Ronald B. Fish has a bachelor of science degree in health and physical education from the University of Minnesota. He is director of wellness programs and services for the Northeast Georgia Medical Center in Gainesville. Ron has been a fitness consultant to the IBM Corporate Wellness Program, and has developed workshops for the YMCA of the USA. In addition, he has hosted his own television exercise program and written a feature column for newspapers in Janesville, Wisconsin, and Albert Lee, Minnesota.

Lawrence A. Golding, PHD, is director of exercise physiology and graduate coordinator for the School of Health and Physical Education at the University of Nevada, Las Vegas. He earned his doctorate at the University of Illinois. Larry was a member and contributing author on a YMCA of the USA research and writing team that compiled the first edition of the *Y's Way to Physical Fitness*, the basic tool for training YMCA Physical Fitness Specialists. Larry has been instrumental in updating that volume as editor for its third edition.